THE MOST IMPORTANT
RELATIONSHIP YOU WILL EVER HAVE
IS WITH YOURSELF.

HELLO,

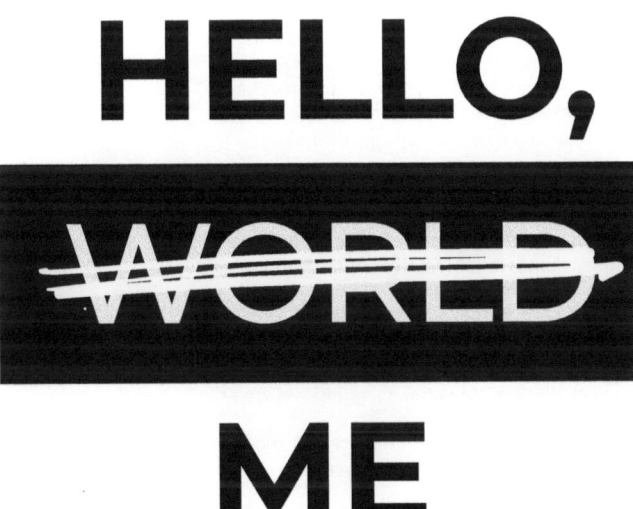

~~WORLD~~

ME

Hello, ~~World~~ Me: A Book of Self-Exploration, Discovery, and Learning
2024 fEmpower Press Trade Paperback Edition.
Copyright © 2024 Lisa Tong

Published in Canada, for Global Distribution by
fEmpower Publications
www.fempower.pub

For more information email: sabrina@fempower.pub

ISBN trade paperback: 978-1-998754-85-4
eBook: 978-1-998754-86-1

To order additional copies of this book:
sabrina@fempower.pub

THE MOST IMPORTANT
RELATIONSHIP YOU WILL EVER HAVE
IS WITH YOURSELF.

HELLO,

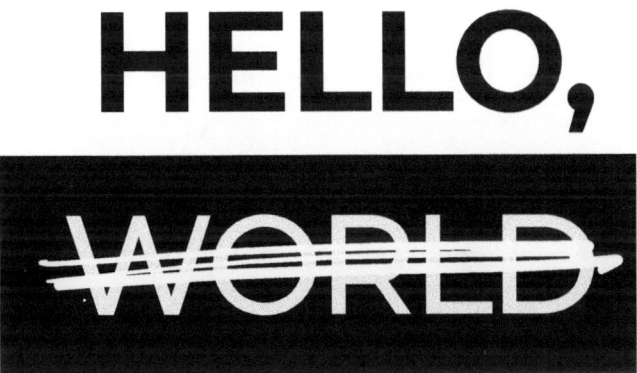

ME

LISA TONG, MBA

THIS PROJECT CALLED **ME**. LITERALLY.

TABLE OF CONTENTS

ABOUT THE AUTHOR

The most important relationship you will ever have is with yourself.

I am an ex-corporate ex-consultant ex-engineer who is passionate about helping corporate women transition **into more meaningful and passionate careers and lives.**

I am a **professionally trained and certified coach** who has coached hundreds of clients, including senior executives, professionals, and students. **I am also a coach trainer**, who established the Canadian branch of an award-winning and internationally recognized coaching school that trains thousands of students each year.

I have been writing and producing content on self-developmental thought pieces for blogs, corporations, and academia since 2017.

Hello ~~World~~ Me is my first book.

Through case studies, where I combine a knack for explaining concepts through diagrams and my teaching experience, I have developed a **self-coaching approach to empower anyone to develop self-awareness, understanding, and growth to create the lives they want.**

INTRODUCTION

Read this introduction the first time you start this book, then go to LET'S BEGIN! next time.

"I wish I had the answers. How come I don't?"
"This is hard. It's just me, myself, and I."
"Do I even know what I want?"
"But I think I know the answers."
"Do I really know?"
"What if I'm wrong?"
"What if I'm right?"
"How will I know?"
"Why am I here?"

Does this conversation sound familiar?

Every day, each of us goes through this type of silent conversation in our minds. We have doubts. We have fears. We have hopes. We have problems. We have dreams. And the whole while, we have a running nonstop marathon narrative in our minds about all of them.

This is what it means to be a human being.

Yet our training, our society, and the world we live in today encourage and reward human doings. We live in a machine of production, competition, and busyness. We are measured by our outputs and valued by our achievements.

At some point in our lives, the human being resurfaces, and we question our human doing parts. We are conflicted. We have different parts of ourselves having different experiences and understanding. We try to hold ourselves in alignment with the rest of the human doers, but our human beings are too strong, and the answers that we thought we had are no longer valid. We struggle to accept what we feel. We begin to question everything around us. We question the way of the world. And more importantly, we question ourselves—which is the best place to be!

A journey of self-discovery starts with questions.

Questions mean curiosity. Curiosity means a willingness to explore and learn. And when you explore yourself, you open yourself up to a world of deeper self-understanding. And when you understand yourself better, you learn to show up, create, and live in a life of possibilities and passion.

To find answers, to find growth, to explore the self, one must start with curiosity.

WHO ARE YOU?

Can you answer this question?
Try it. Write it down.

What do you see?
A title? A description? A story? A narration? A name?
Values? Beliefs? Thoughts? A body?
But really . . . who are you?

This is likely one of the greatest questions you will ask your-self in this life. And depending on where you are in your life, the answer is forever changing. As you experience your life, you evolve. Nothing is ever the same. Not even the cells in your body. Or the thoughts in your mind.

It is the moving target of this question that feeds our never-ending journey of self-discovery. All the questions we ask ourselves can ultimately point to this question.

For example:
"Why am I here?" can point to "What is my life's purpose?"
"What is my life's purpose?" can point to "What am I pas-sionate about?"
"What am I passionate about?" can point to "Why am I passionate about this?"
"Why am I passionate about this" can point to "Well, who am I to be passionate about this?"

Allow all self-discoveries through this book to contribute to your answer of "Who am I?" This is because the answers you discover within yourself, through the support of these tools, will open more understanding on who you are. Slowly, you will discover more and more about yourself, and as you do, you can make more informed and aligned decisions in your life toward the life you truly want to live and to be the person you truly want to be.

THE POWER OF SEEING YOURSELF

WHAT DOES IT MEAN TO SEE YOURSELF?

Seeing yourself means that you can step back from your own mind, your own thoughts, your own subconscious, your own processing, and your own emotions as illustrated in Figure 1. You see these as parts of yourself and develop a new understanding of yourself. This is called self-awareness.

Self-awareness is a very powerful thing to have. It is the gateway to yourself. This is both a skill and a practice. It allows you to see and understand your internal world—and how you interact with the external world.

Figure 1: What it means to be self-aware

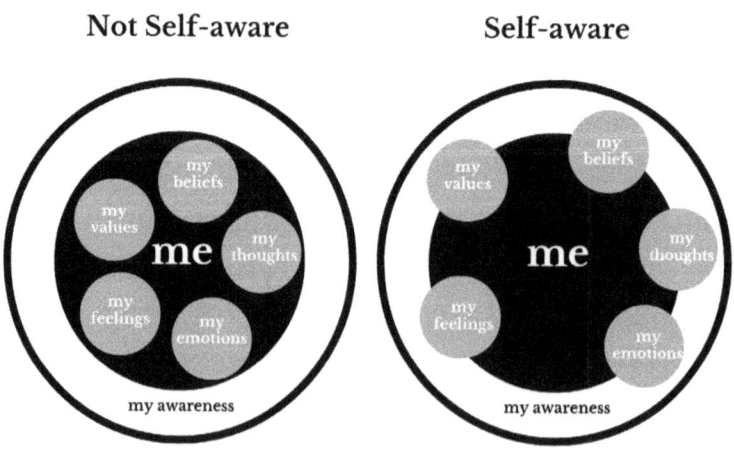

All the gifts in self-discovery come through having self-aware-ness. With this self-awareness, you can create shifts in your own thinking, feeling, and ways of being. This is called having a new or different perspective. Perspective is having an atti-tude and understanding toward something. It is a new way to look at your own experience. It is a new way to look at yourself.

This is what it means to experience yourself in new and dif-ferent ways.

What do you notice about this new way of seeing yourself?
  What is this new experience teaching you?
  How will this learning serve you going forward?

One way to build and practice self-awareness is to capture your observations on paper or digitally. This visual technique is the easiest to work and start with. You can write. You can draw. You can doodle. You can use video or voice recordings. The idea is to be able to see yourself as you experience your thinking and reflection in the moment. The important part of this is that it is IN THE MOMENT. This is the key to creating self-awareness. The gifts in the moment represent your true self. And it is in this vulnerability that you can begin to see your true and whole self.

The best part of this process is that it is with you and you alone. Everything that surfaces is you. Every thought, every emotion, every perspective, every sensation is a part of you.

There is no one else around, except you. There isn't even a real person coach to observe you and witness how you show up. You are with yourself. It is a safe and personal space.

What do you notice about how you are receiving yourself?
Is there excitement?
Is there judgment?
Is there denial?
Is there wonder?
Is there surprise?
Is there . . . nothing?

Allow whatever surfaces to surface as it is. Without judgment. Without reaction. Without filters. This release of control is an important part of truly seeing yourself. It means that you accept what surfaces as a true and raw part of yourself. It is not always the easiest thing to do as self-judgment happens unconsciously in a split second, and sometimes, you don't even realize you are doing it. Use the multiple techniques available to try and capture whatever emerges, especially the parts that surprise you!

HOW DO YOU SEE YOURSELF?

START BY HAVING NO EXPECTATIONS

There exists a large part of ourselves within our unconscious mind. This is the part that we can't readily see in ourselves. It is the part that drives how you think, feel, and behave without knowing it or knowing why. But what if you could see it? Even small parts of it? This is what coaching offers, and this is what self-coaching can offer under the right conditions and mindset that you can create for yourself.

You don't know what you don't know, until you know.

This goes back to the question of "Who am I?" If you don't really know and it's always changing, how valid are having expectations of yourself as you explore yourself then? Expectations are the beliefs that certain outcomes or results should happen. In this way, it is limiting when it comes to self-discovery.

As you embark on this journey, take a lens of welcoming all thoughts, emotions, and understanding. In a way, it is to set your expectations of yourself and the outcomes aside. Expectations are, in a way, a form of self-judgment. What you want to create for yourself in self-coaching moments is a space where you welcome whoever shows up. That is, whomever you are. Because, you don't really know. You will never really know until it shows up.

Expect nothing. Even the expectation that you should have an answer. "I don't know," "Nothing," and silence are also real and valid answers. These are equally useful data points for you to further explore and understand yourself. From nothing, there is something.

You can ask yourself:
- What am I noticing now, as nothing emerges?
- What am I learning about myself in nothing?
- How is this nothing serving or not serving me now?

There is so much to expand out of nothing. Isn't that amazing? So, even from NOTHING, there is SOMETHING. It is not the conscious, logical something you are familiar with, because what does nothing mean? The noun nothing means not anything, not a single thing. And yet, when you connect the experience of nothing in the moment and allow for some deeper reflection beyond the conscious and logical mind, there is something. What that something is, who knows? Not even you, until it shows up! That is what it means to be in the MOMENT and to allow your mind, body, and soul to surrender to whatever surfaces. This is what it means to not have any expectations of how a self-coaching session should go.

The more you know, the more you know you don't know.

I have struggled with my own personal expectations for a very long time and still do to some degree. When I left my corporate role, I felt I had to create projects and become an entrepreneur and be productive with a yearly metric that I had to meet. I felt that I had to have an answer when people asked me, "So, what will you do with your life now?" It took me some time to be comfortable saying, "I don't know what I am going to do with my life."

I had to let go of my own expectations of what I thought I had to become and what I thought I needed to say to the outside world. And through that process of letting expectations go, I have discovered I can do so many different things that I didn't know I could do—like write this book! This is what I implore you to try and do as you go through this self-coaching process. Let all expectations go of how a session should go, or how you think you should respond or feel, or whatever you are thinking now as you read this. Celebrate whatever shows up. As you are.

The most powerful reflective moments happen at the most unexpected times.

WHAT IS SELF-COACHING?

This book is the coach that you need, when you need it.

Right now. Right here. With you. In this moment.

There are times when you need to sort through your thinking and feelings with no other resources around. With the tools found within this book, you can access the resources you need within yourself to become self-aware and make more informed and conscious choices about how you want to move forward and live the life you want. This is the gift of self-coaching. A learning journey.

Self-coaching is a process of self-discovery and learning.

You are the architect of your own life, just as you are the owner of your own life. You are naturally creative, resourceful, and complete. You experience your life in a series of moments. It is with the tools and techniques found in this book that you can access yourself in introspection and find all the answers that you need. While having a conversation with a book does have its limitations, it's designed to mimic the reflective thinking space created in person-to-person conversations.

There are two key things to note in a directed self-coaching experience:

1. There is a defined starting point. Traditional coaching
    does not dictate the starting point, so pick the one that
    resonates with you the most. You will find these in the
    section LET'S BEGIN!

2. There are definitions added so there is a shared under-
    standing of words and their meaning. Most of the time,
    it will be based on your own understanding, but some
    definitions are needed so that you can follow what the
    tool is designed to create.

Self-discovery is not a linear journey. It is about uncovering or
learning something new about yourself in the present so you
can access those possibilities and tap into your full potential
to create the life you want.

**Celebrate the unknown. It is in this unknown
that you will find your full and true self.**

As you embark on this self-exploratory journey, you will discover that:

You can experience yourself in a very different way.
And . . .
All the answers can be found within yourself—always.

While this may not seem obvious, especially when we are so
caught up in our own experiences and emotions, it is there.

As you experience yourself through this book, notice the small shifts in your thinking.

> Did something new enter?
> Did the thought change? If so, how?

Notice the small shifts in your feelings.

> Did they become lighter or heavier or something else?
> Did they change?

Notice how you can see yourself, sitting there, reflecting, thinking, reading, and feeling.

> How are you holding the book?
> With one hand or two?
> Which fingers are on what page?
> What are you feeling?

If you could see thought bubbles floating around you, what would they be?
> Can you label them?
> What color are they?

That's what it means to be aware of yourself. And it certainly does take practice.

**Awareness to the self is a gateway
to the self.**

SELF-COACHING IS DIFFERENT FOR EVERYONE

This book, by design, is self-guided.

What you get out of it is completely up to you. There is no right or wrong way to use this book. There is no right or wrong way to define the success of self-exploration and learning. There is only your way. This book is in service to you!

For some, the book allows for thinking space. For others, it could be the planting of seeds. And for others, it could be a curiosity on developing self-awareness and self-improvement capabilities through the tools found in this book. However you choose to use the tools in this book is completely up to you. Whatever you create is also completely up to you. You are your own master. You are the owner of your own creation.

The self-coaching approach works differently for each person. The pace, the process, the interpretations, the intensity, the depth, and the frequency of reflection or learning will vary by person. This approach begins by exploring your own lens, your own definitions, and your own understanding of yourself and how you see the world around you. It is with this lens that you experience your life and the people around you. This is why two people who are in the exact same situation at the same time in the same place will experience that moment differently as illustrated in Figure 2. It is because we each wear our own lens (Figure 2 smaller circles), which impacts how we interpret, understand, and experience the same situation (Figure 2 outer gray bigger circle).

Figure 2: In the same situation, we will all have different experiences

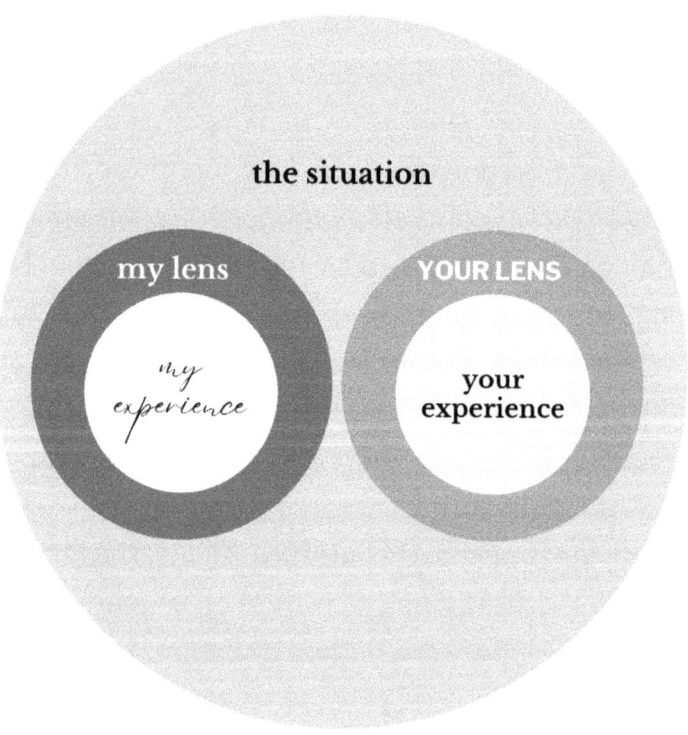

It is this unique experience that is purely yours and yours alone that matters. It is through these experiences and how they shape you that you use as inputs to support you in creating what is possible and positive for you.

THE ITERATIVE LEARNING IN SELF-COACHING

The mind, once stretched by a new idea, never returns to its original dimensions.

A coaching process is designed to create learning and reflections. There are three iterative learning experiences embedded as you go through each tool. These learning experiences are integrated together and feed off each other.

1. Learning about yourself and who you are.
2. Learning how you can apply this learning experience to your life.
3. Learning about how you are learning and evolving how you learn.

Even with the same experience, using the same tool, the learnings and reflections will change for you each time you go through the process. This is because who you are right now will not be the same as who you are ten minutes from now or the same as who you were before you picked up this book. Physiologically, this is also true! Your cells, the water content in your blood, the food in your stomach, and the amount of oxygen in your lungs are all different already as you read this! Each iteration of yourself will experience the process differently because you are not the same person in the same moment.

This is what makes self-coaching so powerful. You can come back to it as often as you'd like and experience something different each time. You can even come back to it without this book. This is because once you've gone through a tool, the process of using that tool—the practice of self-awareness, the process of reflecting, and the experience of asking yourself what you're learning—this is now a part of you. A new you.

Figure 3: Building a new you through a self-coaching process

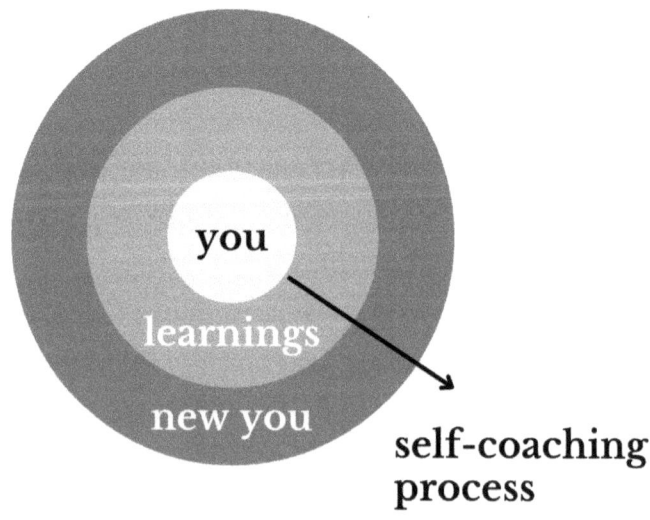

There's you. As you live, there are experiences. Through experiences, there are learnings. The learnings become a part of you. As a result, there's a new you. This is what the self-coaching process enables. And the cycle repeats, forever. You can't stop it. This is the human gift. The ability to learn, whether you choose to or not. It happens unconsciously. Self-coaching puts a spotlight on this process, shifting it from unconscious to conscious. In this, you increase self-awareness, you expand the perspectives you learn, you see more possibilities, and you can intentionally create your way forward.

When you get to the point where you can self-coach with learning moments without this book, congratulations! You have built an iterative learning process within yourself that is sustainable. Continue to generate discovery, growth, and learning from within, because you are resourceful and complete!

This book's mission is to become obsolete. Gift it to someone in need once you've mastered the tools.

HOW TO USE THIS BOOK

USE THIS BOOK LIKE A TOOLBOX!

This book is nonlinear by design. It is not meant to be read like a book, but function as a toolbox where you use the tool that you need for a particular situation. Like how a hammer is intended to allow you to either break things apart with force or very carefully allow you to apply force to a nail, each tool is designed to allow a certain type of expanded thinking and reflection experience. It is in expansion that you can see a part of yourself in that moment. And it is in reflection that you begin to make sense of what you see in yourself in that moment. Each tool comes with questions or positions to reflect on, the opportunity to make self-observations, intentional learning moments, a real case study (where the names have been changed to protect the privacy of my clients) as illustrative, and the theory behind each tool and what it's used for.

Here's the best way to experience a self-coaching tool:

1. Create the right physical environment.
2. Create your mirror.
3. Create the right emotional environment. Give yourself permissions.
4. Formally kick off a self-coaching session with yourself.
5. Where would you like to begin? Pick a statement.
6. Follow the guided self-coaching to the end of the tool.

STEP 1: CREATE THE RIGHT PHYSICAL ENVIRONMENT

Before you start any coaching experience, create the right environment for you to be fully immersed and completely with yourself. Free from distractions. Free from interruptions. The right environment will allow you to step into a more reflective space, allowing more of you to see parts of yourself that you normally can't.

To allow for this, ask yourself:

- Am I comfortable here?
- Does it allow for privacy?
- What is the probability for interruptions?

To create the right environment for coaching:

- Find a quiet and private space for yourself.
- Allow for dedicated and continuous sixty minutes in your calendar.
- Set a timer and don't look at it until it rings.
- Turn off all notifications on your phone, computer, or devices.
- Remove all distractions and keep them out of sight.
- Have signage or announce that you are busy for the next sixty minutes.
- Have water and a snack so you are comfortable.

STEP 2: CREATE YOUR MIRROR

Effective coaching occurs when there is a mirror in which you can see a reflection of yourself. You can see your own thoughts, feelings, and perspectives as they are. The easiest way to do this is by capturing it somewhere so you can see it or replay it back to yourself.

To be your own mirror, you can use:

- Something to capture your reflections on (paper is easiest, but some also like doing voice recordings or digital journals).
- A pencil or pen (if you'd like to get more creative, you can use colored pencils or highlighters).

- The allocated sections of this book.
- The margins of this book.
- The printed worksheets that are available on the website from the QR code at the back of the book.

Tips on being your best mirror:

- Start with a clean page as you come into a session.
- Capture whatever surfaces as it is (even "nothing" is something).
- Do not judge or analyze whatever surfaces.
- Do not edit what you've captured. This is you, in your raw form.

STEP 3: CREATE THE RIGHT EMOTIONAL ENVIRONMENT. GIVE YOURSELF PERMISSIONS.

Willingness is one key ingredient to expand the mind. It is the most important one because as the mind expands, vulnerability increases. An open mind is one that can look past situational, logical perspectives and judgment. It can access narratives, feelings, thoughts, beliefs, needs, and wants from within your mind, heart, body, or soul. It can tap into the subconscious and allow you to step beyond the critical thinker that we are trained to operate as. It can also allow you to step outside of the ego, where we so often judge ourselves and create expectations of who we are and how we think we should show up. As you step into this space, it is analogous to taking your clothes off because your mind is now undressing itself for you to experience. This is why it can sometimes feel uncomfortable. And this is why it is equally important that as the mind expands, it can do so in a safe, sacred space. A space without judgment, without labels, and without expectations.

What permissions do you need to give yourself to be in a safe and open space to be your true authentic self? Ask yourself:

- Is it safe?
- Can I come out now?
- Can I be authentic and genuine?
- What expectations of myself do I need to set aside to truly see myself?
- What will allow me to enjoy this process?

Tips on creating permissions:

- Let go of any and all expectations and outcomes (of yourself and of the session)
  For example, if you are sad and are looking to be not sad at the end of this session, could I suggest letting this expectation go? A coaching session is a learning session and not designed as therapy, even though you may get to the same place eventually. Be open to what surfaces.

- Set clear intentions
Intentions are different from expectations. An intention allows you to direct your energy in a certain direction, whereas an expectation is directed toward a certain outcome.

- Give yourself love and compassion
Step away from a critical and rational mindset toward a mindset of acceptance and love. Love of yourself. Love of who shows up. Love of the process of self-discovery. Through this, you let go of who you think you should be and how you should show up. It doesn't matter right now.

STEP 4: FORMALLY START A COACHING SESSION WITH YOURSELF BY GOING TO LET'S BEGIN!

STEP 5: WHERE WOULD YOU LIKE TO BEGIN? PICK A STATEMENT.

At the beginning, you will explore more reflective spaces, allowing opportunities to think about your own thinking and make observations about yourself. You can take a deep breath first before you reply to any question or even slowly ask the question to yourself out loud. By slowing down your reading pace, you can allow different parts of your mind to come forward. In coaching conversations, the coach controls the pace by the speed of making observations and asking inquiries, but in a self-coaching experience, you can do this yourself with practical and easy techniques such as the one described.

Capture whatever emerges and reflect it as a mirror back to yourself. Normally, your coach would be that mirror for you, but in self-coaching, you can do this for yourself through text or audio or images. Personally, I like to free flow brain dump into a digital journal. This allows my thoughts to surface without filtering or processing, and within these thoughts, I find seeds of myself that I didn't realize were there. The seeds aren't always earth-shattering findings or obvious words. They can be patterns, behaviors, ways of thinking, or random threads.

For example:

- I repeated the word "I wonder" five times in one entry. What about "wondering" was so important for me?
- I used a lot of exclamation marks in another entry. What did the use of the exclamation marks mean? Why did I use so many of them?
- There were a lot of fiery words in one short entry, such as angry, frustrated, on fire, fuming, OH! What, within me, is fueling this fire?
- I found another entry where I kept asking questions: Why is this happening? Why do I feel this way? What is going on? To step back and observe myself asking these questions is self-awareness. I'm then interested to know: What

makes it so important that I have answers to everything right now?

On page 266, I SEE MYSELF—NOW WHAT? you will find a collection of questions that you can ask yourself based on your self-observations. This will expand your ability to see yourself more deeply and further your own understanding of who you are.

One tool that coaches pair with self-awareness is a discovery for learning. Having an awareness is wonderful; however, it feels incomplete unless you can grow and learn from it. This is the "so what?" How will this serve you now going forward? What you do with your learning is completely up to you. In fact, learning can come in all shapes and sizes, ranging from having that seed planted to putting more thought into understanding what it means for you to readily take immediate action. There is no right or wrong answer to learning. Who defines what you should or should not learn? Why must it be defined?

The reflective learning moment is intentionally designed for you to create understanding and meaning about your self-observations.

The last part of each coaching session is to understand and learn what the tool is designed to do. This is a teaching moment. The coaching process is a series of guided intentional questions with inputs and outputs. This book and its tools are the expert of the coaching process. You are the expert of your story and experience. You are the expert of your life. The tools simply facilitate this process.

LET YOUR GUT GUIDE YOU

As you start each session, take five minutes to read and practice through the LET'S BEGIN! section. This section is designed to allow a moment for you to detach from the busy-ness around you (and yourself!) and consciously prepare to go into a self-coaching space.

Your starting point of the session will be based on choosing one statement that rings the most true to you RIGHT NOW in this moment. As you explore the statements:

Which statement resonates with you the most right now?

Which statement draws you to it? Go with your initial instinct.

Trusting your gut also includes keeping an open mind. The more open your mind is, the more exciting the material that comes out of it!

Trust the person you call YOURSELF.

The fact that you are here is a celebration that you are open to explore!

And you will read throughout this book to go with whatever lands first, whatever opens first, whatever pops up first. This is your true and authentic self. There will be moments when the thought, feeling, or way of being isn't what you expected. It is with these unexpected moments, we often unconsciously judge, question, reposition, deny, or justify this in ourselves because the conscious mind is supposed to know who we are, right? However, these are the best sources of insight into our true selves! They are coming from a space that is still you, a space that is authentic—and in a moment when the ego and critical mind are not as active. It is a part of the you that is not carefully curated and crafted for the outside world to see. This is the real YOU. Don't judge whatever surfaces. Just allow it to surface and become aware that it exists—in you! It is a part of you! As you practice accessing these parts more and more and become aware of them, you can begin to look at who shows up versus who you think should show up. This is illustrated in Figure 4 on how this self-exploration also includes challenging truths.

Figure 4: Who shows up versus who you think should show up

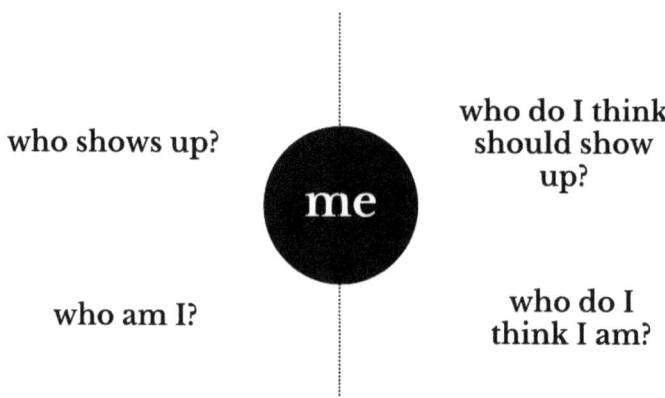

What are you noticing about all the parts that are emerging?
  What do they mean to you?
  What do they mean ABOUT you?
  How does this allow you to think about who you are?

Remember to take breaks.

When you see this:

-
-
-

It means to pause. It follows a question or a moment to reflect. This is intentionally designed so you don't skip ahead of the process.

Self-discovery is a lifelong journey.

START HERE

(if it's your first time here, go back to the INTRODUCTION)

LET'S BEGIN!

The most important relationship you will ever have is with yourself.

Taking the intentions to step into a self-coaching session is a wonderful gift to yourself. The best part of this is that you don't even know what the gift is at the end!

As you begin, take a few moments now to actively center yourself.

Read this section first and then practice this centering exercise at your own pace.

Drop your shoulders, relaxing them.
Relax your tongue, dropping it from the roof of your mouth.
Soften your jaw, releasing the muscles around your face.
Close your eyes.
Picture a safe and comfortable place in your mind. I like ocean-sides with bright blue skies.
Where is your safe and comfortable place?
Inhale slowly through your nose, counting to three, and then slowly release your breath through your mouth, counting to three again.
Do this breathwork three times.
Open your eyes and continue.

Now, think about:

What do you want out of today's session?
What would best serve you today?
What do you need to let go of momentarily to allow space for yourself?

You can write this down if it helps or keep it in the back of your mind. It is nice to revisit this at the end of your self-coaching session to check in on progress. It doesn't need to be big and grandiose as we often think change should be. Something like "I'd like to sort my thoughts" or "I'd like some clarity" or "I'd like to feel differently about . . ." or "I'd like to spend some time with myself." This is more an intention rather than an expectation. It is the directing of energy rather than the concrete creation of an outcome.

Take five minutes now to get centered and reflect on your own intentions for this session.

-
-
-

The next piece is important because it is your starting point of the coaching session. As you aren't in a normal bilateral open coaching conversation, there are nine tools to choose from as a starting point.

Pick the one that resonates the most with you right now.

Which statement resonates with you the most right now?
Which statement draws you to it?
Go with your initial instinct.

Are you ready?
Go to page 36, WHERE WOULD YOU LIKE TO BEGIN? PICK A STATEMENT.

WHERE WOULD YOU LIKE TO BEGIN? PICK A STATEMENT.

If you haven't read the section LET'S BEGIN! start with that to get grounded first.

Now, take a few minutes to read through each statement below in Figure 5: Where would you like to begin? Pick a statement.

You are the source of your creations

Ask yourself:
Which statement resonates with you the most right now?
Which statement draws you to it?
Go with your initial instinct.

Figure 5: Where would you like to begin? Pick a statement

Which statement resonates with you the most right now?	Go to page . . .
I have an idea!	37
I feel sad.	60
I feel angry.	71
I have fears.	103
I am stuck.	171
I am lost.	181
I don't know.	194
I can't do it.	224

I HAVE AN IDEA!

LEARNING OBJECTIVES OF THIS TOOL:

- Develop a self-awareness for your own inner sparkles that ignites ideas.
- Strengthen your sparkles as self-anchors.
- Develop a plan to move forward.

If you haven't read the section LET'S BEGIN! start with that to get grounded first.

You have an idea!
This is exciting!
Ideas are the outputs of your creative and abundant self. This is where the magic starts!

Remember, don't rush through the questions. The slower and more intentional you are about reflecting, the more valuable the observations.

Take a few moments now to take three deep breaths and think about your idea.

Now, let's capture this idea.

The intentional blank page (next page) is for you to capture this idea in whatever form calls to you. It can be in writing, in colors, in pictures, as a diagram, or as a series of words. You can also download a template of this worksheet from the QR code at the back of the book.

As you do this exercise, dump it out as it is.
Don't judge it.
Don't analyze it.
Don't critique it.
Don't box it.
Don't clean it up.

What we want is to allow your genuine and full creative self to reveal itself.

What is the idea? Use the next blank page to capture it.

-
-
-

Once you are done, take a step back and sit with this. Take the space to the right margin on your idea page to capture your reflections for the next two questions.

What excites you about this creation? Use these prompts to help you.

Through this creation:

I feel . . .
I become . . .
I can . . .
I am . . .

-
-
-

As you reflect on this excitement, see it as sparkles. Big, bright, and shiny sparkles.
What within you makes it sparkle? What is it within you that is behind this inspiration?
If it helps, close your eyes and turn inward. Do not rush this part. There is something in you that is driving this excitement. There is something that is making it sparkle.

-
-
-

You can read each excitement statement and ask this question to yourself: "What within me is sparkling this?"

Write the first answers that come to you in the reflection section.

Just capture it.

-
-
-

Now, synthesize this down into one to three key words. Words that represent that sparkle. The word(s) should make you feel powerful, excited, and engaged. It doesn't matter what the word is, only what it represents for you.

-
-
-

These are your anchors. Your excitement anchors. It is not the idea or the process of creation, but what allows for your excitement to emerge. This is the root of your energy. What you create is only the output! You are a source of your own creation.

Use this excitement and what keeps it alive as anchors.

This is where self-awareness starts. It is to recognize the excitement and why it sparkles so much for you.

Take a moment now to give your anchor the spotlight. This means placing it front and center and in your awareness as often as possible.

What would be a powerful way to be reminded of these anchors? For example, you could write them on sticky notes and put them on your computer. You could create a phone screensaver. You could write them on your mirror. You could keep a note in your wallet.

-
-
-

SO, WHAT NOW? IF YOU'D LIKE TO CONTINUE WORKING THROUGH YOUR IDEA, YOU CAN GO TO PAGE 260, NOW FOR A PLAN . . .

IF YOU DON'T KNOW HOW TO MOVE FORWARD, GO TO PAGE 50, I HAVE AN IDEA, BUT I AM STUCK

CASE STUDY

Brian was finishing his final year doing a full-time MBA at the Hong Kong University of Science and Technology. I worked with him on building his résumé and profile as he looked for full-time employment. He also spoke of a vision to build something on the side as a part-time gig.

We met once every two weeks to discuss his progress and every time we met, he would circle back to his dream of being an entrepreneur.

"What makes it important to be an entrepreneur?" I asked during one of our sessions.

"It seems like the thing to do right now and I really want to try this," he replied. "A lot of my classmates are in this space, and we had a venture capitalist visit us last month and I was very inspired about what they said about how ideas can turn into value creation."

"I can see some of the external influences, such as it's the thing to do now and that your classmates are all building on their own ideas. And then there's this very important internal piece in you of wanting to try and you being inspired to create value," I said, reflecting on the two parts of how his story was showing up.

He nodded.

"What is that inspiration you speak of to create value?" I asked.

I could see his eyes widen and light up, and he straightened himself up in his seat.

"Oh! I want to create something that is unique, that is healthy and will excite busy people in food and beverages." He shared the various ideas that he had for creating a series of meals and drinks designed for students and busy people. He was very excited about the products and passionate about the lifestyle his brand would represent.

"I can see how excited you are about this. I would love to know, what is it within you that is behind this inspiration?" I asked this question intentionally slow.

He paused and looked up for a moment.

"I know what it's like to be so busy that you don't have time for healthy meals, and it's important for me to maintain a healthy way of living. I'm not getting any younger, but I want to feel and stay feeling younger. I want to inspire others that they can choose healthy lifestyles as well, even if they are super busy." And then, he spent the next ten minutes resharing his idea and how it would change the world.

This was his anchor. This was his why.

For his homework that week, I invited him to spend thirty minutes writing his idea down in its rawest form directly from his mind. I instructed him to write without fear and judgment of the idea and simply write as much as he possibly could in that time frame and not stop until the thirty minutes were up.

This would be the start of a beautiful journey of Brian becoming an entrepreneur. Over the next few months, he refined the idea and had a prototype out by the end of the school year. However, throughout this process, he was not without doubts and roadblocks.

"My parents keep telling me I should focus on school and get a real job," he told me during one of our sessions.

"That's definitely a perspective," I said. "And how does this sit with your anchor?"

"It doesn't." He frowned. "I can get a real job and do this at the same time."

Or another time, he shared with me how he participated in a venture capital pitch competition and was discouraged because he didn't place. We explored what he learned from the experience and then, I asked, "How does this learning affect your anchor?"

"It doesn't. It actually made me see what I needed to do differently, but the anchor is the same."

It was important to establish awareness and understanding in Brian of what his excitement was and what was feeding it. This allowed him to create a mental anchor and continually come back to it when he didn't know how to move forward. It allowed him to see his own sparkles and redirect his energy in moving forward toward building his dreams.

TEACHING MOMENT

Anchors are important parts of ourselves. Some of these anchors are values, beliefs, or attitudes, to name a few. They are characteristics within us that form our mindset and how we show up in the world.

This excitement anchoring exercise is important to do periodically as we work on different ideas in our lives, whether it's a project idea, a process idea, or any ideas. Ideas don't need to be big; it can be anything, even the idea to bake a batch of cookies or the idea to go for a walk. The key is to be aware of the sparkle that exists inside of you— that's self-awareness. When things are internally driven, they stick. It is because we own them. They belong to us and within us. We control what happens to that anchor, and we can choose how we want to use it.

When we are excited about something, we invest energy into it. When you pair excitement with an idea, it can move mountains.

You can revisit this anchoring exercise any time you want to inject energy back into what you want to create. There will be moments when you feel deflated, unmotivated, or in doubt. Allow these feelings to wash over you, but don't let them linger. Think about your anchors. Allow your energy to be redirected and keep creating what excites you.

Everything you need is from within.

FIVE QUESTIONS TO HELP YOU FIND YOUR ANCHORS:

1. What excites you?
2. What would you like to create as a result of this excitement?
3. What is it within you that is behind this inspiration? This is your anchor.
4. What would one word be to capture this inspiration?
5. How will this anchor serve you going forward?

I HAVE AN IDEA
(WORKING PAGE)

You can use this space for your guided coaching session for page 37, I HAVE AN IDEA! It can be in writing, in colors, in pictures, as a diagram, or as a series of words. You can also download a template of this worksheet from the QR code at the back of the book.

What is the idea?

What excites you about this creation? Use these prompts to help you.

Through this creation:
I feel . . .
I become . . .
I can . . .
I am . . .

Create your anchors: What is it within you that is behind this inspiration?

I HAVE AN IDEA, BUT I AM STUCK

LEARNING OBJECTIVES OF THIS TOOL:

- Explore unrestricted flow on how to move forward with an idea.
- Develop self-awareness of how play can increase your flow.
- Create and experience a space of flow.
- Develop a plan to move forward.

When work is play . . . you become limitless.

You have an idea, but you are stuck.

It's time to play. Really play.

This exercise allows you to be wildly creative in how you show up for yourself.

The objective is to commit to fifty-five minutes of uninterrupted playtime with your idea. This playtime is exactly that—play. It is not a moment of analysis, prioritization, or judgment. It is simply play.

You will spend:

1. Thirty minutes to play with as many statements as possible starting with: **"To move forward, I can . . ."**
2. Ten minutes to play with ten more statements.
3. Fifteen minutes to reflect.

What you'll need:

- Your idea and anchors (from the "I HAVE AN IDEA!" session)
- Pieces of paper, sticky notes, or a digital journal
- Pen or pencil
- A quiet space
- A timer

How to create a blackout space for yourself:

- Find a quiet moment in your calendar for fifty-five minutes.
- Set a timer and don't look at it until it rings.
- Turn off all notifications on your phone, computer, or devices.
- Remove all distractions and keep them out of sight.
- Have signage or announce that you are busy for the next fifty-five minutes.

The best way to play:

- Go crazy—seriously. There is no limit.
- Give yourself permission to play. Openly and honestly.
- Consider "If I had all the resources in the world…" how would you answer differently?
- Don't judge or analyze anything right now.

Have you seen small children at play? They just play. No matter the idea or scenario, they don't judge or criticize each other. They build on top of each other and become even more excited as they collectively build. In their world, everything is possible.

Imagine that space right now.

Take a moment now to review your idea and your anchors. You can keep this page open beside you as you play.

READY?

GO!

Write as many of these statements as you can. Don't stop to think—just write!

To move forward, I can . . .

-

-

-

Once you are finished, take some time to reflect on what you've just captured.

How did you feel about unrestricted play?

-

-

-

What did this activity allow you to create?

-

-

-

What is different about this way of creating versus how you normally create?

-

-

-

And now, what you do with the list is completely up to you!

If you've found a way to move forward, go to NOW FOR A PLAN on page 260.

If you're still feeling stuck and not energized, you can go to the "Five Tips to Stimulate Flow When You're Stuck Moving an Idea Forward."

However, if you're feeling stuck and not energized, take a break at this point and come back to this exact exercise tomorrow. Seeds also need germination time, and sometimes, you can't rush creativity. However, take a moment to celebrate this session. Acknowledge the time, effort, and personal commitment it takes to get to this point.

CASE STUDY

"How many ideas do you think you guys can generate collectively as a group?" I asked, as the facilitator.

The challenge was delivered.

The answers ranged from twenty to fifty.

This Regional Finance team had sixteen members. There were four teams of four members each. We were on day two of a series of half-day team-building workshops. Today, we were tackling how the team could improve communication with their stakeholders.

The current task: Come up with creative ways to engage their stakeholders.

Each group had stacks of single colored sticky notes. Yellow, green, blue, and pink.

The objective was to write as many ideas as possible, as a team, to address the task within fifteen minutes. They would then stick them on a wall and the team with the highest unique idea count would win.

It started out slow, each team discussing the ideas collectively, and someone scribing. But as the walls began to fill with colored stickies, the competition heightened. Multiple scribes emerged, each team formed sub teams, some teams formed a line to the wall, and some gathered at the wall. The room was charged with an excited creative energy.

"Five minutes remaining," I called out.

The volume of stickies doubled in the last minutes of the activity. It was incredible to watch! The teams no longer discussed feasibility of the idea or how to resource the idea, they simply produced. And no idea was too crazy. They were in it to win.

By the end of the session, Team Yellow had 20 unique sticky notes, Team Blue had 35, Team Green had 37, and Team Pink had 42. For a grand total of 134 ideas. Even if the ideas had overlaps between the teams, they almost tripled their initial projection.

The teams reflected on what happened.

"We wanted to win, so we weren't paying attention to the quality of the ideas, we were focused on quantity."

"The five-minute call-out created a sense of urgency. I think it was at that time that we felt an increase in outputs. Everyone was madly writing ideas and sticking them on the wall. It was fun!"

"It was like we had permission to go crazy . . . we weren't even checking for overlaps or feasibility. Any idea was a good idea!"

The learning was that they reached a point of uninhibited creation. They released judgment of themselves and of each other. The criteria of the quality of the ideas disappeared and the teams simply created. This idea of implicit permissions emerged, and it energized the teams collectively. They were playing.

TEACHING MOMENT

We are very good at filtering ourselves. Our brains do a phenomenal job of automatically checking raw thoughts against our own lens, which is the lens of our values, beliefs, and attitudes. This is why sometimes when we have ideas, by the time we share them out, even to ourselves, they have already passed through our multiple lenses. One way to bypass these lenses in a self-coaching situation is to overload them. You can tire out your brain and filtering system.

This is what this exercise does. You continue to push it

until the filtering either becomes tired or irrelevant. You find yourself ignoring personal judgment and criticism as you enter into a state of genuine and uninhibited play. It doesn't matter what comes out. It only matters that it does come out. Because if it doesn't come out, you can't see it. Allow everything to come out and enjoy it.

This is also known as being in a state of flow. The energy now used is to generate and create, not judge and filter. This is living in possibilities. However, there are moments when we are really just stuck. There is no more flow. Next are five tips to push flow further:

FIVE TIPS TO STIMULATE FLOW WHEN YOU'RE STUCK MOVING AN IDEA FORWARD

1. SET A DIFFERENT TARGET.

What are the target criteria for flow to happen? How did you come to define it? You run out of flow because there is an expectation that the product of flow needs to look a certain way. What if you set different and unexpected criteria for flow?

In I HAVE AN IDEA, BUT I AM STUCK on page 50, you used time as the criteria for flow, nothing else. It doesn't matter the idea or thought, you flow, flow, flow until time runs out. Another one is the number of statements or sticky notes produced. For example, you must produce fifty stickies before you can stop flowing. Or allow flow to run through the alphabet from A to Z and each idea has to start with that letter.

2. MAKE IT FUN!

Creation should be fun. When you're in a space of pure excitement and joy, it becomes enjoyable. That's play. You can make it competitive, you can gamify it, or you can create rewards for it.

3. ASK CHILDREN. OUTSOURCE IT.

Literally. Hand off a simplified version of your idea to them and see what they can create. Allow them to freely explore your ideas. Sometimes, you are your own limit. Allow these to be launch pads for reigniting your flow.

4. SET CRAZY CRITERIA.

How many undoable ideas can you produce? This is giving permission to not be perfect. It is intentionally pushing your expectations of quality to the opposite end. How many ways forward involve using animals? How many ways forward start in the middle? Stop thinking linearly and logically. This is hard to do, so use crazy prompts to drive creativity.

5. CHANGE UP THE WAY IT FLOWS.

If your flow is through a certain medium, such as writing, change it to drawing. There are many forms of flow such as audio (storytelling, singing, or breathing), visual (crafting, journaling, or filming), physical (movement or stillness), or anything that comes to mind. Change it up from within. You can access different parts of yourself through this shift. Each part of us has a different lens in how it shows up as you, so let these variants emerge and create in their way.

Remember, the world looks pink when you're wearing rose-colored glasses. It doesn't mean you can't wear these lenses, though there are times when you should take them off. It is first having an awareness of the lenses that you wear, and second, training yourself to change lenses that serve you better in the moment.

NOW IS A GOOD TIME TO GO TO PAGE 242,
WHAT ARE YOU LEARNING NOW?

I FEEL SAD

LEARNING OBJECTIVES OF THIS TOOL:

- Experience your sadness fully.
- Develop self-awareness of how the sadness shows up physically.
- Explore the parts within you that emit sadness.

If you haven't read the section LET'S BEGIN! start with that to get grounded first.

Can you truly feel and appreciate your sadness first? Don't dissect it. Don't analyze it.

You feel sad.

This is such a beautiful thing to acknowledge and experience.

Sadness.

Sadness is an emotion. It is a part of being a human being. It is a part of the human experience.

It is important to recognize that you feel sad right now.
Sit with it.
Let it wash over you.
If it's useful for you, write down your answers on a separate
piece of paper.

What permissions do you allow yourself right now to fully
embrace and feel your sadness?

-
-
-

Emotions emerge as physical sensations in our bodies. This
is how it shows up unconsciously. For example, sadness
can show up as tears, a tightness in the chest, a lump in the
throat, ringing ears, quivering lips, increased blinking, shallow
breaths, weak knees, itchy palms, or whatever that is for you.
This is how your sadness shows up.

Close your eyes and feel where this sadness feels the strong-
est in your body. It can be in one part, multiple parts, or all
parts of your body.

Take as long as you need to feel it all.

What part is that?

-

-

-

As you feel the sadness here, how is it showing up in this part? There is no right or wrong way to feel the sadness. Simply feel how it shows up here and allow it to come through. Does it tingle, hurt, twitch, feel cold or hot, move, tighten, sweat, shake, contract or expand, freeze, itch, or something else?

How is the sadness showing up in this part?

-

-

-

This is good to acknowledge. Learn how your sadness shows up through your body and physical senses. These signs inform you that this feeling exists, and this awareness allows for choice.

You can choose to let it run its course. You can choose to be still and listen to what it is saying. You can choose to interrupt it. You are conscious of your choice and what serves you best in this situation.

Emotions are sign posts. They are trying to tell you something. This is the practice of listening to yourself.

Take a moment to do just that. Listen to yourself. Listen to the sadness.

What do you think this sadness is trying to tell you by showing up like this?

Let whatever shows up, show up.

-
-
-

Based on this, what do you want to tell the sadness?

-
-
-

Nicely done. Up to now, this was all about allowing you to experience the sadness for what it is. A feeling. A temporary feeling that will pass. And a chance to interact with it.

Did you find this session challenging?

-
-
-

If so, take a pause and reflect on what made it so challenging.

-
-
-

If you felt that this session was challenging, there are six techniques to try to thoroughly experience your sadness in the Teaching Moment of I FEEL SAD.

GO TO PAGE 242, WHAT ARE YOU LEARNING NOW?

CASE STUDY

Belinda came to me as a client while she was experiencing multiple significant life changes. She had recently moved back to Canada with two teenaged daughters from Hong Kong. She was adjusting to carrying a full-time job on top of handling a household and doing chauffeur duties. Her dad was recently in a serious accident and her husband was in between countries managing his businesses.

She spoke often of how all her pots were "overboiling," and yet when I asked how she was really doing, she would reply, "I can do this." She would sit up straighter in her chair and repeat, "I can do this."

"How are you feeling about your 'I can do this'?" I asked during one of our fortnightly sessions.

"I feel sad. I feel sad that this is not the life I expected or wanted for myself. But—" and then she would continue to explain that she could do it and shared with me her prioritization techniques. We usually ended these sessions with pragmatic and practical takeaways for her to carry on.

On another occasion, she shared with me her frustrations of her marriage. "I feel abandoned," she said. And then she'd go on to explain what was causing this frustration.

I noticed that Belinda was able to speak about feeling her emotions from a logical perspective, but not truly process and feel them. She was exceptionally good at explaining her emotions and narrating them.

Until one day, as she spoke of her overboiling pots again,

she started crying. "Give me a moment—" She waved at me through the camera, reaching for a tissue. This was her go-to phrase when she wanted to reign it in.

"Belinda, I am here with you," I said, reassuring her slowly and intentionally. "Would it be so bad to not take a moment now and just be with your tears? Let them come."

She paused and looked at me. I could see her thinking as she blinked and looked away. "No . . ." She started hesitantly, then sighed. "No . . . no . . . it wouldn't be bad." Her second and third "no"s were softer.

This was the permission she needed to fully embrace and feel her sadness. I prompted it, but she needed to give herself permission to go there. The remainder of this session was spent on challenging her need to regroup and come from a logical head space. We explored what she was experiencing between allowing more heartspace into the conversation instead of headspace, and through this, she could feel her emotions rather than talk about them as an entity. She could own them. She could acknowledge they were hers. She could experience them and thus, process them as something passing through her rather than outside of her.

TEACHING MOMENT

Sadness is like rain. Emotions are like rain. They have a time limit in which they serve a certain purpose. They, too, shall

pass. Rain has its use for the earth. It creates rivers. It nour-
ishes. It sustains life. Look at sadness in a similar way. There
is something that it is offering us or else we would not feel
it otherwise. This is a part of the human experience.

To feel sad is healthy and normal. We learn from the polar-
ities of ourselves, like a pendulum. How will we understand
happiness if we don't feel the opposite? I encourage you to
capitalize on this opportunity, but don't dwell in it. Experience it enough to grant yourself the moment, but do not
allow it to imprison you.

Here are six ways you can practice feeling emotions,
rather than thinking about feeling them. Try the ones that
connect with you the most first. Not every method works
for everyone.

SIX WAYS TO THOROUGHLY EXPERIENCE YOUR SAD

Start by ensuring you're in a safe and personal space to be
vulnerable with yourself.

1. DO A FULL BODY SCAN WITH IT.

Take the sadness and feel it from the top of your head to the
tip of your toes. Let it wash completely through your body
as if you are taking a paint brush colored sad and painting
yourself. Notice where it sticks the most.

2. BREATHE THROUGH IT.

Take deep, slow breaths in through the nose and out through the mouth. As you inhale, picture the sad entering your body. As you exhale, feel the sad exiting your body. Allow it to balloon and deflate through you.

3. CRY.

Do not underestimate the power of crying. And do not judge yourself as you cry. There is a common self-limiting belief that crying is weak or shameful. In fact, allowing yourself to cry is a strong position. Crying is the physical release and experience of an emotion. You cry to release the tension in your body. It is necessary and healthy.

4. DUMP IT OUT.

Some people feel the sadness more deeply when they can hear or see themselves in a safe space. It is like a form of release. Write or say it out loud to yourself in full details without filtering it.

5. CONNECT WITH YOURSELF.

This is a form of meditation. Give yourself full permission and your undivided attention to reach into your mind, body, thoughts—your soul. Let the sadness lead this connection into yourself. There are many techniques to support this, such as guided verbal meditations, music, sounds, breath work, yoga, and many more that allow you to come into a state of self.

6. CONNECT WITH OTHERS.

There is power in experiencing sadness with people we trust. Let them know about what you're experiencing and ask for what you need, which is often just a pair of ears. "I am sad right now. I would love for you to simply listen and be here with me, please." This request is very powerful because it sets the expectations up-front. You are not looking for solutions at this time. You are simply looking to be heard.

Thinking about feeling sad is not the same as feeling the sadness. When you feel sad, feel it. Do not think about why you are sad, what's causing the feeling, how to stop it, or how badly it feels. Stop thinking about it. It's a hard thing to do because your brain is naturally trained into solving mode. Let all expectations go of what you should do with the sadness. Do nothing and the feeling will emerge.

**NOW IS A GOOD TIME TO GO TO PAGE 242,
WHAT ARE YOU LEARNING NOW?**

I FEEL ANGRY

LEARNING OBJECTIVES OF THIS TOOL:

- Develop self-awareness of how the anger shows up physically.
- Learn about the perspectives you see in anger.
- Learn to circuit break yourself when the anger is leading you.
- Develop a self-regulation process to manage the anger.

If you haven't read the section LET'S BEGIN! start with that to get grounded first.

You feel angry.

Oh, you have come to the right place with this experience.

You feel angry.
There is a lot of energy in this statement.
  Can you feel it?

Describe this feeling of anger. What image comes to mind? Capture as many characteristics as possible. Give shape to this feeling. You can use the following page to work through your observations.

-
-
-

For this next question, you don't have to answer right away. Allow yourself to feel it.

Take three deep breaths before you move on. As you breathe in through your nose, count to three and breathe out through your mouth. Do this three times and really allow yourself to feel it.

Where do you feel the anger? Notice where it burns the hottest within your body. It could also be in multiple places.

-
-
-

This is a good start. This is one way to observe the self in this "feeling angry" experience. Emotions often show up as physical clues in our body. Some people clench their fists when they are angry. Others clench their jaws. Some will feel a tightness in their chest.

What are you learning about yourself in where you feel the anger in your body?

-

-

-

Now take a moment and consider whether the anger is leading you or if you are leading the anger. There is no right or wrong way to experience this right now. It is simply who you are in the moment. Anger is temporary. It is only a signpost to something more within you. Allow it to emerge as it is.

When the anger is leading you, it considers only "me" and in a frame of loss.

Frames of loss sound and feel like:

- I don't have . . .
- It is difficult . . .
- I won't . . .
- I can't . . .
- Something is missing . . .

If at this time that is all you can see, the anger may be leading you. For example, "I can't do it" or "I'm losing it" or "This is the worst situation possible." If you are leading the anger, it considers a wider circle of impact. For example, "Perhaps my partner is seeing it this way" or "If I did this, then it would impact my team in this way."

So, keeping this in mind . . .

At this point, do you feel that the anger is leading you or you are leading yourself?

-
-
-

This is an important question because if the anger is leading you, then decisions are anger-led (or emotionally driven) and often lead to unintended consequences. We do and say things that are in support of the anger only and not in support of a creative process, which creates value for ourselves and those around us.

IF YOU FEEL THE ANGER CONTINUES TO LEAD YOU, GO TO PAGE 84, THE ANGER IS LEADING ME . . .

> **IF YOU FEEL YOU ARE BACK TO LEADING YOURSELF, GO TO PAGE 89, TAKING A MOMENT . . .**

CASE STUDY

I want to share the story of Ned, who is a senior executive at a software firm.

He came to me with the same experience of "Oh, I am feeling angry!" in two separate coaching conversations, yet with very different moments of decision-making readiness. In this case study, Ned demonstrates both being anger-led and leading the anger on two different occasions. This was my second formal coaching session with Ned, so the relationship was still relatively new.

The first was that he had just gotten off an important performance review with his boss. I happened to be scheduled immediately after it. I am not sure whether this was intentional or not on his part, but it allowed me to experience him at the height of his "I am feeling angry!" emotion.

And, oh boy, was he angry! He didn't need to say it. I could see the tension in his curled fists, the quickened pace of his breathing and talking, his choice of words around the situation, and I could feel the tension emitting from him like he was on fire. I allowed and supported him to download as much as he needed. This lasted for fifteen minutes. I asked what he would like to have happen at this point and he shared how he was going to rewrite this performance review, demanding what he deserved, and to have another meeting with his boss. Rather than work with him to solution through the anger, I asked him to feel the physical sensations of his anger right now. He was puzzled by my request at first, taking a pause and furrowing his eyebrows at me. He later admitted to me that he was expecting something completely different, but went with it anyway. This process allowed him to start building the muscles of self-awareness and deeper self-understanding. He never paid attention to this before, but he was smart and sharp and immediately understood where I was going with this. It was another tool in his self-management toolkit, and once he understood, he could also teach others. It was a wonderful observation! As we closed the session, I checked in on what he would like to have happen again. He paused first and said that he would have to sit with it first and come back to me. He wanted some time to strategize the best way to do this without coming off ungrateful and angry. Not only was he able to pause on making decisions that were anger-led, he wanted to also use this as a coaching tool for his teams.

The second time he came to the coaching conversation with the experience of "I am feeling angry!" it was from a situation that happened earlier during the day. He was still feeling angry, but it was from a place that something at work was still unresolved. He had planned a way forward with how he would manage this with his team and the messaging he wanted to give to his boss around doing what was best for the company. He was in control of the anger rather than the anger leading him. He self-managed into a calmer state emotionally before we met using the new tools he had learned, and we spent quality moments unpacking his own understanding about this type of feeling of anger and its connection to unresolved work items. I didn't coach him through the situation but allowed him to see himself in the experience and how he understood himself better from within.

TEACHING MOMENT

Emotions are like signposts as much as they are like rain. They are part of our human response to something in need or off balance. That is where it offers value as signposts. They are also temporary and have a time limit to how long they exist. Like rain, it will pass in due course.

Often, when we recognize an emotion, we are already deep in it. Anger is a great example of this where the anger overwhelms us before we even know it. Some don't even realize they are angry until it's too late and something unintended has happened. This is what anger creates. This need to remove, eliminate, or get rid of what it is that is making us angry, whatever that may be. And we move into fight-or-flight mode. This is the instinctive way of managing anger. We see this in children who become angry and react to it the only way they know how, such as jumping up and down, crying, or other behaviors that they have learned. This is not wrong. It is simply how the internally unregulated and anger-led body and mind process this emotion and show up externally.

Learn to feel your feelings. They are teaching you something.

This is not to say you can't feel anger. In fact, you should feel these emotions. All emotions! If they are signposts, then feeling them will allow you to understand what the sign means. And sometimes, it takes a while longer for you to read the signpost—especially if it's got a lot of small words—and decipher it. This is an important step in self-coaching. This initial step of self-awareness will allow you two things: the first is a deeper understanding of yourself through this experience, and the second is the time and space to come into a calmer state of mind and have more control of the choices you make around this experience. Feeling the emotions and reacting on them are different and separate actions. Yet, so many people blur them together because of how quickly one leads to the other.

Welcome to self "circuit breaking" 101, as illustrated in Figure 6. This intentional self-awareness practice will enable you to insert a conscious break into that blurry part of feeling anger and doing something you didn't intend to do. While anger exists as an emotion in our mind and heart, it also manifests in and through the physical body. Each of us are wired differently, so take note of where this feeling exists in your body. This is a good indicator that when you feel that part of your body start to burn, you could be moving toward this feeling of anger. This noticing act is the circuit breaker. Once you can break the automatic transition of feeling anger to doing something unintended, you can create different outcomes, similar to our case study. Once Ned was able to recognize the physical sensations associated with anger, he could circuit break the anger-led decision-making and shift toward a state that served him better.

You can do this session multiple times to use these as data points to look for patterns. These patterns then inform us of our default behaviors and how we show up unconsciously.

There are many tools and techniques available to you once you can circuit break yourself between feeling anger and reacting to that feeling of anger. You can go to page 89, TAKING A MOMENT to learn any of these tools and techniques.

Figure 6: Circuit breaking yourself when you feel anger

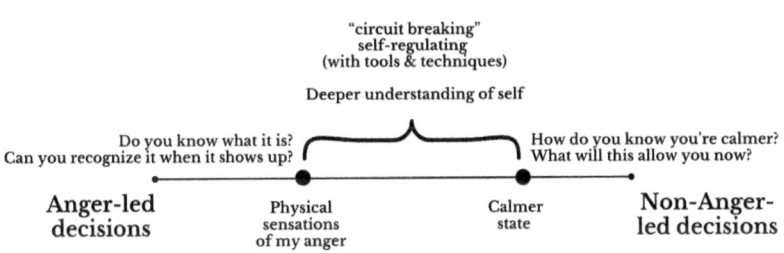

"circuit breaking"
self-regulating
(with tools & techniques)

Deeper understanding of self

Do you know what it is?   How do you know you're calmer?
Can you recognize it when it shows up?   What will this allow you now?

Anger-led   Physical   Calmer   Non-Anger-
decisions   sensations   state   led decisions
                 of my anger

You can use a "circuit breaking" technique to shift from anger-led decisions (the anger is leading me), to non-anger-led decisions (I am leading the anger). It starts with understanding what the physical sensations are in the body when you feel anger. The next time you feel these physical sensations, pause to understand what is happening, and circuit break the anger with self-regulating tools and techniques to shift to a calmer state of mind to allow you to make choices that create value for you and those around you.

I FEEL ANGRY
(WORKING PAGE)

You can use this page for your guided coaching session from page 71, I FEEL ANGRY.

Describe your feeling of anger. What image comes to mind? Capture as many characteristics as possible. Give shape to this feeling.

Where do you feel the anger? Notice where it burns the hottest within your body. It could also be in multiple places. You can use the little person image to guide you.

TEACHING MOMENT

These physical sensations are how anger shows up in your body. Pay attention to them and repeat this self-coaching session multiple times to collect data points about yourself. Once you recognize these, you can then learn to "circuit break" your anger as these physical sensations show up and create different outcomes for yourself that is led by you, rather than led by your anger.

THE ANGER IS LEADING ME . . .

This is good to recognize. It is a good place to be. Right here. Right now. Especially as you realize the anger is still leading you.

Since you're here and not in the experience that has caused your feeling of anger, you're actually in circuit breaking mode. You have consciously made a choice to pivot away from anger-led decisions, even though the anger is still leading you.

Think on this for a bit. You are here. You have made a choice to come into a book during a state of feeling angry.

Going forward, you can either think it through in your head, or if it's useful, capture it on paper or a digital journal.

Where is the anger leading you?

-
-
-

For this next question, a neat way to increase self-awareness is to ask yourself this question by reading it out loud. Do it slowly. Do it intentionally. Allow yourself to explore you in a different way.

Ask yourself out loud:

"I am here with a book right now. Why am I so sure that the anger is leading me versus me leading myself?"

-
-
-

This question invokes taking personal accountability. It challenges you to reflect what you can observe about yourself in this state of anger and acknowledge it.

What are you learning about yourself now?

-
-
-

Well done for getting this far. Exploring a feeling, particularly the emotion of anger, is not easy.

Where are you now with regards to the anger leading you?

Feel it again.

-
-
-

IF IT'S STILL LEADING YOU, GO TO PAGE 89,
TAKING A MOMENT . . .

IF YOU ARE NOW LEADING YOURSELF, GO TO
PAGE 98, I AM LEADING MYSELF . . .

CASE STUDY

Let's continue the story of Ned, a senior executive at a software firm who I was newly engaged to work with. I was hired to support underperforming executives with an objective to integrate organizational feedback into growth opportunities for both the individual and the organization.

During our first coaching session, Ned came to me with an "Oh, I am feeling angry!" experience. He had scheduled this coaching session immediately after a performance review with his boss.

For the first fifteen minutes, he shared an "I" perspective in frames of loss.

"Yes, I am angry!"

"I am very disappointed in this organization."

"There are clear issues with the team."

"I feel robbed."

"I deserve more."

I allowed him the space he needed and supported him through this moment. It allowed him to both physically and emotionally process what was needed. The steam. The anger. The feelings.

While in this state, his course of action was to rewrite his performance review and demand what he deserved. This is anger-led decision-making.

We focused on the physical sensations of his anger in his body for the remainder of the session. This allowed him to circuit break his anger and shift into a state of increased clarity.

At the end of the session, he didn't have a final way forward—yet. But he did have a clearer perspective that he would need to further strategize the best way forward.

TEACHING MOMENT

When water boils and you try to see yourself in its reflection, it is completely distorted because of the bubbling water. This is the same as trying to see yourself in states of anger. There is too much disturbance to be able to see yourself and the situation clearly. As a result, you are working with distorted information in a singular perspective that may not serve you best.

There is nothing wrong with this perspective. It is you experiencing yourself in the situation at the current moment. It is important to allow this to surface for what it is and let it run its course. There are two intentional perspectives here in this tool. The first is the use of "I" in the question. This is you stepping outside of yourself. This is being self-aware. It is you asking yourself. Taking accountability for your feelings and your actions is an important step in self-growth.

The second is to challenge what you think you know about yourself. Feelings aren't always truth. They are simply signposts. Acknowledge, accept, and evaluate them. You don't need to hold on to them. They don't define you. They aren't you.

TAKING A MOMENT . . .

This is a good moment to be here.

You feel angry.

You've managed to circuit break yourself from taking any anger-led decisions, which is great self-awareness in practice and illustrative of your ability to take control. This is very good.

You still feel that the anger is leading you, which is perfectly normal. There are these moments when it needs more time to process.

This next part is more teaching than self-coaching. These tools help you process the anger that is still leading you to get to leading yourself.

Before you begin, there is one important question for you to consider. Read through this carefully first and then ask yourself the question again. This question challenges you to become self-aware of your changing states.

The question is: At what point will you know that the anger is no longer leading you?

As explored in the I FEEL ANGRY tool, when the anger is leading you, it considers only "me" and in a frame of loss. If you are leading the anger, it considers a wider circle of impact with clarity of yourself and your situation.

Now ...

At what point will you know that the anger is no longer leading you?

-
-
-

This is part of being self-aware. It is also an indicator that the conscious effort you're investing in yourself is working. You can try any of these techniques and come back to the book to finish up if you'd like to go into a self-learning space.

SIX TOOLS FOR MANAGING ANGER IN THE MOMENT

To manage the anger in the moment is to delay action. It is to gift yourself with time to see yourself clearly in choice so that you can create the outcomes that serve you best. Anger has the loudest voice when it shows up. Managing it is not to dismiss the anger, but to give equal voice to all of you. Not just the anger in the moment.

1. CIRCUIT BREAK IT, FIRST.

One great way to introduce the circuit break is to recognize the physical sensation of the burning and then to hold a pause. Check in with the sensation and feeling. Once you can circuit break, your choices are unlimited. How do you want to intentionally move forward from here?

2. ACCEPT THIS FEELING AND ALLOW IT TO WASH OVER YOU.

You can say, "I feel angry right now" and do what you need to privately process it. You don't need to justify or explain anything. You don't even need to understand it. Sometimes, you just need to be with it and allow it to run its course in a safe and private space where you can be yourself.

3. DOWNLOAD IT SOMEWHERE SAFE.

To download means to allow a release of your thoughts or feelings in its rawest form.

A safe place is where only you can see them or access them. It could be a diary, a journal, a voice recording, or anything else meaningful to capture it. Safe also means that you recognize it is one part of you speaking. The anger part. Not the whole you.

I like digital journaling. I type fast and furiously, spilling whatever is on my mind in that moment. I talk to myself. I complain. I swear. I ask questions. I am in victim mode. But the release of it is very powerful. It is what I need to process the feeling. And then, I will go into my self-coaching process when I know I can lead myself again.

This can also work with a trusted friend. It is important to establish the premise of the download with them. You could set the tone by saying, "I'd love for you to be my ears right now. I'm angry and need the support of a nonjudgmental, safe space. Could you be this for me now?" In this, you are also teaching them what you need. No assumptions. No solutions needed.

4. REMOVE YOURSELF FROM THE SITUATION.

Take a moment to gently step away if you can. It could be taking a walk, leaving the room, turning off your video for a few moments, or even requesting for space and to not engage in conversation. It could sound like, "I'm sorry, I'll just need a moment for myself right now. Thank you."

5. ENGAGE IN ACTIVE BREATH WORK OR MEDITATION.

Breathe deeply and slowly. Focus on the slow, steady inhale and exhale of your breath. Notice the temperature of the air as in enters your nose or the shape of your mouth as it exits. You can use counts of three. Alternatively, I also use guided and musical meditation to regulate my breathing. Save your favorites so they come in handy when you need them right away.

6. USE PHYSICAL DISTRACTIONS.

You can engage in physical activity as a distraction. Drawing circles on a page, coloring, playing with a fidget toy or the piano, cooking, and going to the gym are several ways to engage the body to allow things to settle. I prefer these to be solo activities so that I know I don't potentially do or say anything I may regret later.

Well done.

As a part of continued developing self-awareness and self-learning, reflect on what techniques work for you and why. This will allow you to consciously build a muscle of intentional circuit breaking until it becomes unconscious and a habit.

What technique did you use?

-
-
-

How did you feel about using this technique?

-
-
-

What are you learning about yourself now?

-
-
-

How will you know you are leading yourself? Well, check in. Are you there now? If you are, you can now go to page 98, I AM LEADING MYSELF . . .

If not, that is OK. Continue to take the moments you need.

CASE STUDY

I have learned throughout my own self-awareness journey and growth that two of my physical triggers, when I am angry, are a tightness in my chest and tears. I will feel the tightness in my chest first like I want to pop and then the tears will inevitably come after. It's a combo meal. I can understand this in myself as a part of paying attention to how my body reacts when I was going through a few years of very difficult personal challenges.

When I experience the tightness in my chest and I allow myself to cry, I will take a private moment to journal it out. It becomes a writing marathon where I madly type whatever comes to mind.

My journal entries are littered with more profanity and spelling mistakes than I would like. I have learned to not care. This is how I show up in these moments of fully feeling the anger and not worrying about how I show up or being careful of what I express. It all comes out—raw and unfiltered. And I always ask myself this one question: What would I like to have happen instead? And a barrage of feeling-sorry-for-myself perspectives emerge, which sometimes fuels my anger, but I let it. I am feeling powerful and enraged. However, I eventually do run out of steam, and it is at that moment, I know I have shifted to leading my anger instead of the other way around.

I recognize this when:

I have stopped swearing.

I use less exclamation marks.

I see frames of gain instead of frames of loss.

I feel the tightness in my chest has dissipated.

I stop crying.

It has taken a year of practice with journaling (and data points) to the point where I can do it in my head as a running narrative. The important part of circuit breaking from an anger-led to a self-led perspective is when you can recognize the shift. It is here that I know I can see more clearly on how to move forward without hurting myself or others with the decisions I make and how I show up.

TEACHING MOMENT

It is OK when emotions lead us. It happens. Sometimes, it is necessary. We experience this when we feel angry. It is loud. It is in your face. It is the main actor in our story. However, it is in how we manage that moment and what we can learn from it that matters. And we can't learn without experiencing it.

Emotional maturity is the ability to acknowledge, accept, and process the experience of the emotion in a healthy way. This includes accepting that we are still processing it. In our fast-paced, results-driven world there is an expectation that we shouldn't show our emotions or that leaders should be level-headed. We put everything else above our own emotions and tell ourselves that is it OK. Emotional suppression is a part of burnout. Emotional suppression is self-neglect. This doesn't mean we are in a constant state of anger or sadness or even happiness. That is not possible. It means we respect our emotions and what they mean for us as human beings.

Take the moments. Whether they are anger, sadness, or happiness. Allow the emotion to process and run its course.

I AM LEADING MYSELF . . .

When you are back in control of yourself, this is a good sign the feeling of anger has run its course as much as needed to allow you to be in a calmer state to make more creative and loving decisions in your life.

Emotions are like rain. Let them pass as they should.

"I am leading myself."

This is a powerful statement.

For this next section, write down your observations as a part of continued self-discovery and building self-awareness.

What within you allowed you to step back into leading yourself?

-
-
-

What are you noticing about the feeling of anger now that you're leading yourself?

-

-

-

Well done in stepping back and making observations about yourself, both in the moment of feeling anger and in the process of taking control back in leading yourself. This is practicing self-awareness.

You went from feeling anger to circuit breaking and pausing to consciously taking control back of yourself in an emotional experience. And to top it off, you're also now conscious of what that power is within yourself to do that.

It is amazing.

Truly. To get this in a matter of a few pages in this moment is truly beautiful.

You can create something different here for yourself.

You are in control of your decisions and your life.

You have the power to take back control—always. The emotions are temporary, as illustrated just now in this experience that you're having.

Well done.

**AT THIS POINT, YOU CAN GO TO PAGE 242,
WHAT ARE YOU LEARNING NOW?**

TEACHING MOMENT (WITH A CASE STUDY)

You feel emotions because you are trying to tell yourself something. The emotions do not materialize from nothing. And to recognize that experiencing all emotions across the human spectrum is normal and healthy.

You are whole and complete as you are. Sometimes, we are simply blocked from accessing our own wholeness and who we are by ourselves, our limiting beliefs, or our own thinking. We are in our own way more often than we realize. It is in this reflective self-coaching exercise that you become more aware of the power you can wield to access your completeness and wholeness in the different parts. And sometimes, there's a key. Feeling emotions is such a key. This is why the emotions exist. Emotions are signposts. They are part of our human response to something in need or off balance. They are part of the human experience.

No emotion is felt forever—even ones that we enjoy such as happiness or pleasure. This means emotions we enjoy less, such as sadness or anger, also won't be felt forever. The first step is to allow yourself to truly feel and not suppress, dismiss, or diminish these feelings, especially anger.

Anger is a signpost that there is something we do not accept about ourselves.

There is something there within you that is giving rise to this feeling of anger. While you may think it is externally stimulated, there is something within you that is attracted to this external stimulus to create this feeling inside. Perhaps some truths? For example, if someone said to you that your blue hair was very unattractive and that you looked like a clown, but you don't even have blue hair, what would you think? Would it connect with you? Would it feel different if someone said to you that what you were wearing was ugly? If you truly loved what you were wearing, you were confident in it, and you knew you looked smoking hot, you'd brush it off and think they were delusional and maybe think, *That's not nice.* However, if you thought there was some truth to what they were saying, maybe a seed of doubt that you don't match or an inkling of insecurity around how you looked, it may create a stir of emotions such as anger or sadness or something else not so uplifting. And it is perfectly OK to feel whatever that emotion is and to be self-aware to circuit break yourself before you react, especially if the feeling is anger.

There are two techniques shared to grow your self-awareness as a result of experiencing "I feel angry":

Pay attention to the physical sensations in your body as you experience the feeling of anger. Use this as input to learn about yourself and how these emotions show up physically for you.

With these points of data about yourself, you can now understand your own coded behaviors. Any time these behaviors or physical sensations show up, you can choose whether to circuit break or see the emotion through, and then be aware of your choices in how you show up and make decisions. This is truly standing on the outside of yourself and seeing you in your thoughts and behaviors.

I HAVE FEARS

LEARNING OBJECTIVES OF THIS TOOL:

- Develop self-awareness in your own definitions of fear versus what causes a fear.
- Own your fear and set intentions with it.
- Learn about your own limiting beliefs and how to overcome them.
- Develop strategies to live courageously and boldly with fear.

If you haven't read the section LET'S BEGIN! start with that to get grounded first.

You have fears.

With deep fears, deep love also exists.

This is a great recognition to have. To be able to see and acknowledge the fear is an important step in self-awareness and personal development. Having fears is very normal. We all have fears. This is what it means to be a human being. And it is through these fears that you can learn and grow in yourself.

It is also important to acknowledge your readiness to come into this space.

The ability to have deep fears is paralleled with the ability to have deep love. Keep that in mind as you work through yourself and your fears.

As you work through this section, allow whatever surfaces to come fully to the surface.

There is no one here, but yourself. Observe what emotions surface. Observe what triggers appear. Observe reactions and hesitations. Observe yourself in all of it.

There is power in seeing all the fears for what they are and how you experience these fears. It starts here, like this, right now.

Ready? Take a few deep breaths before you begin.

Take as long as you need. Go as slow as you need. Be as thorough as you need. These are not easy questions and will take a bit of introspection to answer. If it helps, you can write these answers down to reflect back on later.

What is it that you fear?

-
-
-

What makes this fear a fear for you right now?

-
-
-

Well done.

The important thing here is to recognize that "what makes this fear a fear" is something that you can identify and that exists as a part of your reality. It is a part of your current truth.

For "what makes this fear a fear" right now, pick the statement that resonates with you the most.

I HAVE EXPERIENCED WHAT MAKES THIS FEAR, A FEAR. GO TO PAGE 110, I HAVE EXPERIENCED WHAT MAKES THIS FEAR, A FEAR.

> I HAVE NOT EXPERIENCED WHAT MAKES THIS FEAR, A FEAR. GO TO PAGE 153, I HAVE NOT EXPERIENCED WHAT MAKES THIS FEAR, A FEAR.

CASE STUDY

"I'm having trouble with my teenage son," Donna said. "He comes and goes when he pleases, he doesn't clean up after himself, and it's so hard to predict if he's going to have dinner with us or not after I've prepared everything."

Donna's a single working mother with a younger daughter and a teenaged son. She came to me for professional coaching, but today she felt it was pertinent to table a more personal matter, which I welcomed.

"He's rude, disrespectful, asks for money when he needs it, and doesn't contribute to the household chores," she said, then let out an exasperated sigh. I could visibly see her agitation.

We continued to explore her son's behaviors until I asked this question, "What would you like to have instead?"

"I'd like for him to show some respect. I'd like for him to contribute and be a part of the family. I'd like for him to take care of his sister." The list was extensive.

"This is good thinking for your role as a mother. I'm curious, though. Is your son aware of these?"

"No, I'm too scared to tell him." She looked sheepishly up at me with her head slightly bent down.

"You're scared to tell him," I repeated with intentional slowness. I was intentional not to use the word fear if she didn't label it as such, although some would argue being scared and having a fear are the same thing. Are they though?

She nodded.

"What makes it difficult to tell him?"

"I'm scared of his reaction. I'm scared I'll push him further away."

"Thank you for sharing, Donna. I hear that you are scared of telling your son his responsibilities in case it will create more distance in the relationship."

She nodded.

"And I also hear that you have not had this discussion with him on your expectations of him as a son and a member of the household?"

She nodded again.

"What makes this true that you will push him further away if you share your expectations with him?"

Donna frowned slightly and furrowed her brows in thought. "Oh . . . I don't know for sure . . . I mean, I think just based on his behavior in and around the house. I don't think he will take my suggestions well."

What was Donna's fear? She feared speaking frankly and directly with her son about his responsibilities to the household.

What was causing this fear? She didn't want to create more distance with her son.

Has she experienced what was causing her fear before? No.

We further explored her thinking here, unpacking some of the assumptions she made and accessing a creative space where she could step up to be the mother she wanted to be without letting her fears get in the way.

TEACHING MOMENT

Fears are a part of us. We all have fears. This is what it means to be human. Some fears exist consciously, ones that we recognize and see, such as having a fear of heights or a fear of lions. These fears are biological in nature to keep us safe. They exist for survival purposes. Some fears exist subconsciously. Ones that we didn't know were there, until we truly began to understand ourselves in authentic and egoless ways, such as a fear of rejection. Some of these subconscious fears are also meant to keep us safe and whole. Safe psychologically, safe emotionally, safe internally. However, when these fears are present and continue to lead and control our lives, they become anxieties. And then crutches.

Recognizing a fear as a fear is a tremendous acknowledgment for a human being. It is leaning into vulnerability. The real gift is to be able to unpack the fear and see how we interact with and experience it. We are complex beings and often, the fear is embedded in this complexity. It is not so simple to look at a fear, identify what makes this fear a fear and banish it. If it were only that easy! This is where the tools of self-coaching and reflection can enable an open and curious individual to explore their own fears further and find the opportunities to grow and expand above and beyond the fears, redirecting energy to create meaningful and positive ways to live with or through the fears.

Do not let the fear lead you. Instead, redirect that fear in search of love and creation for yourself because that capability exists.

I HAVE EXPERIENCED WHAT MAKES THIS FEAR, A FEAR

This is great recognition in how this is a part of you. You have experienced it.

Experience teaches and shapes us, and yet, it doesn't have to define us.

Take a moment to reflect on this current experience.

When you think of what makes this fear, a fear . . . what part of you experiences it?

A part is how you define it. It can be physical, spiritual, mental, or something else. The key is to know that it is a part of you. It is a part that you recognize. It is a part you can define.

-
-
-

Take a moment to sit with this part, whatever it is, and just be there with it. This is a safe space.

Which statement resonates now around what you'd like to do with this?

Pause to read each one, then select the one that connects the most with you right now.

1. I want to overcome.
2. I want to reframe.
3. I want to let go of.
4. I want to avoid.
5. I don't know.

IF IT FEELS LIKE "I WANT TO OVERCOME," GO TO PAGE 113, I WANT TO OVERCOME.

IF IT FEELS LIKE "I WANT TO REFRAME," GO TO PAGE 124, I WANT TO REFRAME.

IF IT FEELS LIKE "I WANT TO LET GO OF," GO TO PAGE 129, I WANT TO LET GO OF.

IF IT FEELS LIKE "I WANT TO AVOID," GO TO PAGE 142, I WANT TO AVOID.

IF YOU PICKED "I DON'T KNOW," GO TO PAGE 194, I DON'T KNOW.

TEACHING MOMENT

Experience teaches a lot. We learn and remember more through experience than through textbooks or lectures. This is no different to how we then perceive and react to fears and what causes the fears that we have experienced. We project this experienced learning on to future situations and sometimes let it control us. However, these experiences don't have to define us. We can create the narrative around these experiences. We can accept or reject how experiences are imprinted on us.

I WANT TO OVERCOME

This is a very bold and proactive choice.

What you've done is intentionally chosen something different for yourself. You've chosen to acknowledge, understand, and cultivate a new mindset and attitude to create the life you want.

You are not your fear. You are only experiencing your fear. And you can change your perception on your own experiences.

This is what you have done.

This is what it means to be resourceful and creative as a whole person. And you have access to these parts of you. It is wonderful!

As you consider your fear and your desire to overcome it . . .

What would you be able to create if, for one split moment, you were braver than your fear?

-
-
-

What is this "overcoming" narrative from within you now? Write down this narrative. It is very powerful to see how you are showing up for yourself now.

-
-
-

What excitement is created because of this overcoming?

-
-
-

What makes it important that this narrative exists now?

-
-
-

This is your story now. Remember the excitement. This is how you have chosen to move forward in your life toward possibilities.

I choose me.

This is what this tool is supporting you to strengthen. Keep this story alive and in a safe place where you can revisit it again and build on it. This is the start of a great and beautiful journey. But more importantly, it's the start of realizing your full self-potential in creating the narrative and life you want.

With this narrative, how will you move forward now?

-
-
-

What is different about your fear now?

-
-
-

This is how you've taken your intention of "I want to overcome" and transformed the energy away from being held back by your fear to conquering it.

What, within you, will keep this "overcome" narrative alive?

-
-
-

Well done. Truly. No matter how small or big this power is, it is yours. And yours alone. It comes from within. Take a moment to review what you've discovered.

IF YOU FEEL THIS "OVERCOME" IS COMPLETE FOR NOW, GO TO PAGE 242, WHAT ARE YOU LEARNING NOW?

IF YOU WOULD LIKE TO CONTINUE STRENGTHENING YOUR "OVERCOME," YOU CAN GO TO PAGE 120, SIX TOOLS TO OVERCOME FEARS.

CASE STUDY

I have fears too. Many of them!

These particular ones started with the bold move of quitting my corporate life of twenty-plus years.

More specifically, it was the weekend when I was planning to submit my resignation the following Monday. I had my resignation letter typed, dated, and signed. I had my resignation email sitting in my draft outbox. I had an alarm set for 9:00 a.m. Monday morning to remind me to do this very important task.

Yet, I was so scared.

I feared pulling the plug.

Follow me as I walk through this "I have fears" tool with a very strong desire to overcome this fear so I could follow through and live the life I've always wanted.

Q: Lisa, what is it that you fear?

I fear quitting a comfortable and consistent life that I've known for so many years. It is familiar space. I fear the unknown.

Q: What "makes this fear . . . a fear" . . . for you . . . right now?

I fear the unknown because I am a person of low risk. I like stability. I like predictability. I like data. I like planning and doing scenario analysis on outcomes. I like being in control of my life.

Q: Have you experienced what makes this a fear, a fear before?

Yes, although not often and not in this scale. I understand that we can't always be in full control of our lives. I can't control other people. I can't control outcomes. I can only control how I react, how I think, and the narrative in which I experience my life.

Q: What would you be able to create, if for one split moment, you were braver than your fear?

I would be able to create all the things I love. I would be able to share my love of soup making and helping those find their passion (as I have). I would be able to create a life that I've envisioned that is driven by doing something I am truly passionate about at this phase in my life with flexibility and mobility.

Q: What is this "overcoming" narrative from within you now?
I am the true architect of my life. While I don't have all the data and information at every moment of my life, I know that I have the skills and ability to navigate whatever comes my way. This is what I've wanted for a few years now. I've built up enough momentum across a few small businesses and it's now time to shift my energy to what excites me the most. It's time. It's now.

Q: What excitement is created because of this overcoming?
I have the time, space, and capacity to create and build the things that excite me the most! It's writing this book. It's creating the platform to help people to follow their highest level of excitement. It's making Chinese soups and creating content to improve health through soups and herbal teas. It's so many things! I get very excited when I am in creation mode.

Q: What makes it important that this narrative exists now?
This has been a dream of mine for so many years. And I've recently moved to a new role where things have been challenging. I know I could have continued to invest energy into my corporate role and make things work, but I was questioning whether this was the best way now to invest my energy. And the answer was NO. It was time. I knew.

Q: What, within you, will keep this "overcome" narrative alive?

I journaled my "overcome" narrative and wrote meaningful prompts on yellow stickies and stuck them on the wall above my computer. Expressions like "This excites you!" and "It's time to go all out and just create!" continue to inspire me from within. I now continue to follow my highest level of excitement. This is now my modus operandi. Even creating a website is exciting now!

This helped me to overcome my fear of sending the resignation letter. I used this "overcome" narrative as fuel when my alarm rang at 9:00 a.m. on Monday morning and I sent that email.

I had other fears that emerged after that, such as the fear of having that conversation with my manager. My "overcome" narrative continued to serve me and I used that as an anchor to hold course, stay professional, and see it through.

Q: What am I learning now?

I learned that my fears were holding me back from living to my greatest possibilities and potential. I learned that the power to overcome came from within myself. I learned to follow my heart more and my head less. There were so many lessons as I continued to experience fear, acknowledge it, and know that these fears didn't define me. The greatest learning here is that without the fears, I didn't know I had this within me.

TEACHING MOMENT

Fears either protect you or trap you. Both are valid perspectives because they exist for you and from within you. But they are not you. They don't define you. They don't control you. It may feel this way sometimes, but when you take a stand to overcome your fears, you are taking a step toward silencing the part of you that is holding you back.

When you choose, you take responsibility for yourself into your own hands.

SIX TOOLS TO OVERCOME FEARS (OR WHAT CAUSES THE FEAR)

1. START FROM A PLACE OF ABUNDANT THINKING RATHER THAN LACK THINKING.

Lack thinking is a mindset that sounds like "if only . . ." Abundant thinking is a mindset that sounds like "even if . . ." or "what if . . ." This means, what if the fears didn't exist; what is possible? If you could have, create, or source whatever it was you needed at that moment to move toward what excites you in life, what would that be? What do you already have and know that can overcome this fear? How would you show up differently if this fear did not exist in this form? How could you turn what you do not want into something that is useful to you?

To practice abundant thinking, rephrase your thoughts with:

- Even if . . .
- What if . . .
- . . . yet. (Add a "yet"to the end of your sentence.)
- . . . soon. (Add a "soon" to the end of your sentence.)
- I get to . . .

2. WRITE IT DOWN.

Capture your fear in explicit detail. All of it. Where you can see it. And then, just sit with it. Explore yourself fully in this form. What are you noticing about the fear? What are you noticing about yourself as you review it?

3. REWRITE YOUR CURRENT AND FUTURE NARRATIVE.

This allows your mind to push beyond its current limited think-ing. You can't create what you can't see. So go ahead, write it out first. No matter how ridiculous or far-fetched you think it is. That is, you judging what is possible. Try this exercise with no limitations at all. What does it feel like to be completely free of your own mind? Your own fears? Your own boundaries?

4. DIRECTLY CHALLENGE YOUR FEARS.

Show yourself that your fears have no basis of truth. Ask yourself: Is this true? Am I absolutely sure? How am I so sure? Pay attention to which parts of you begin to argue with yourself.

5. USE THE FLIP TECHNIQUE.

You want to flip each fear so that you can see what it will unblock or allow. It sounds like, "I overcome the fear of . . . in order to create . . . in my life" or "If I overcome my fear of . . . I will create . . . in my life." You can use this tool as a summary from these tools, keeping these statements short, yet powerful.

6. DRILL DOWN THE WHYS.

Unpack your fears using "why." This technique will help you see deeper than the fears. It can help you unlock beliefs or limiting beliefs, values, and perspectives you didn't know existed. Keep drilling until you can drill no more. It can become cyclical, which is when you can stop. And repeat this as often as you need because every time you go through it, something new may emerge.

For example:

I feared submitting my resignation. Why?
I feared giving up a stable and steady income. Why?
Because I feared the unknown. Why did I fear the unknown?
Because then I lose control of my life. Why do I need control of my life?
Because it keeps me psychologically safe. Why do I need this?
Because maybe I am lacking in other areas of my life. Ouch.

Every drill down is a part of me. A different part of me, but they are all me. There is nothing you need to do with this right now, other than see it and understand that it exists. And now that you have awareness, you have choice.

After each tool, take a moment to go to page 242, WHAT ARE YOU LEARNING NOW? This will help you anchor what you're observing about yourself with the tools.

I WANT TO REFRAME

Reframe in this context is to change the way you see the fear.

Based on this, think about . . .

What positive impact will this have for you to reframe?

-
-
-

Being here in the mindset to reframe is a big win.

It is something you want for yourself (with "I").

It is something that creates possibilities in "reframe."

This is a very proactive choice on your part.

You are not your fear. You are experiencing fear. And you can change your perception of your own experiences.

This is what you have chosen to do.

This is what it means to be resourceful and creative as a whole person. And you have access to these parts of you. It is wonderful!

As you reflect on your fear . . .

List all the ways that this fear can help you create what you want. You can use these prompts to guide you:

"Through this fear . . . it has taught me . . ."

"Through this fear . . . it has allowed me to . . ."

"Through this fear . . . it has created for me . . ."

For example, having a fear of public speaking has taught me to take a moment before I go on stage to center myself. Through this centering, my thoughts are clearer and more organized as I take three deep breaths to calm myself.

What is the new "reframing" narrative now about your fear? Write down this narrative.

-
-
-

What excitement is created because of this reframing?

-
-
-

What makes it important that this narrative exists now?

-
-
-

This is your story now. This is your new and shifted perspective. Remember the excitement. This is how you have chosen to move forward in your life creatively and lovingly toward possibilities.

And with this newly reframed story, how will this serve you going forward?

-
-
-

AT THIS POINT, GO TO PAGE 242, WHAT ARE YOU LEARNING NOW?

CASE STUDY

Let's play a game.

It's called "Can you spot the difference?" between my two stories.

I am a skeptic of people. I believe that when given the opportunity, people will show up selfishly and meanly. I will say "Good morning" to everyone I pass on a run. There were two who did not reply to me. They were so mean. If I see them again next time, I'm not offering any greetings. This is highly discouraging. Why should I put out effort when other people don't? No one says "Good morning" to me first.

Alternatively, I believe that everyone comes from a good place. I believe that when given the opportunity, people will show up positively. I will say "Good morning" to everyone I pass on a run. On average, the return rate of replies is around eight out of ten. That's fantastic! Maybe the 20 percent didn't hear me or are too shy to respond. And that is OK. It doesn't deter me from sending out my free morning cheers.

Both stories have the exact same data points. What's different then?

TEACHING MOMENT

You live in the narrative that you create. Your perception plays a big role in how you live your life, how you react, and how you make choices.

You are the creator of your own life.

Yes, you may be born into circumstances, but you have free will. While you can't always control external factors, you certainly can control internal ones. You can control the stories you tell yourself. You can create the narrative you want. You can build a mindset of possibilities.

In a reframe mindset, you are not letting go of it. You are not changing data or facts. Instead, you are rewriting whatever you did not want to be replaced by something you prefer. You are making the old mindset redundant. This is a very powerful ability. You are taking full responsibility for yourself and what happens in your mind. This reframe happens internally, recognizing that the external remains the same.

I WANT TO LET GO OF

Letting go of is to release yourself from self-created imprisonment.

It is to say that the fear does not control you.

Its existence does not matter.

You can feel it. You can see it. You can sense it. You acknow-ledge it. But it does not define how you should feel, react, or live because of it.

This is a very conscious and intentional choice to make.

Take the time to slowly go through these reflective questions. Capture them on paper so that you can see the definitions and markers you have created for yourself.

When you say to let go of, what does that let go of mean?

-
-
-

How will you know it's been let go of?

-
-
-

This is your marker. It is important to note it down so that you can know whether you've let go or not.

With this next question, close your eyes and feel where the attachment exists. There's a cord there. It could be a physical, emotional, mind, soul, thinking, or any part.

This "let go of" . . . what part of you wants to let go of?

-
-
-

This is important to recognize. It is only a part of you that is holding on and now wanting to let go of. It is not the whole of you. It is not really YOU.

What makes it important that this part lets go of?

-
-
-

What will allow this part to let go of?

-

-

-

This is really good work. You know what to let go means. You know how you'll know you let it go. You know which part wants to let go and why. And you know the enablers.

How will the parts that aren't attached now support the part that is attached to let go?

-

-

-

And with new understanding of letting it go, how will this serve you now going forward?

-

-

-

YOU CAN NOW GO TO PAGE 242, WHAT ARE
YOU LEARNING NOW?

CASE STUDY

"I want to genuinely help people," my heart piped up. It wasn't my physical heart speaking; it was the heart of my soul. I didn't really know what it was at the time, nor did I understand what it meant.

"OK, fine, you can explore a coaching course," a part of my head, my logical brain, conceded. "But you can't quit your day job."

Fast-forward to three years later. I became a certified coach. I built my own coaching side business. It excited me. I was happy doing this. My heart was happy. There was still that part of me that knew I wanted to let go of my corporate role. But my head could not and would not let it go.

I knew what my anchors were. I could feel the divide within me between what I really wanted to do and what I thought I had to do. It is this tension that is the telltale sign for a need to challenge my beliefs.

Why does the tension exist?

What is the tension telling me?

Why do I struggle so much with the two sides?

Knowing that I was working with a set of limiting beliefs, I used the gentle power of my own excitement to slowly convince (or trick) parts of my brain to challenge these limiting beliefs and deconstruct the parts of my value system that I was holding on to.

For example, to be successful at school, I had to be an engineer, accountant, or doctor. I chose engineer. To be considered successful in a career, I had to work at a multi-national organization. Art was only a hobby. Piano was mandatory. And I was celebrated for my job title and how much money I made. These were my limiting beliefs. Beliefs that I have carried since childhood from immigrant parents.

I challenged these beliefs. I observed real-life cases that countered these beliefs. I began to reframe my narratives, little by little. Eventually, my value system was flipped upside down so the brain did not recognize or understand what it was holding on to anymore. And so, with a tiny pang of panic, but a bigger bang of excitement, the brain let it go. I quit. I resigned from corporate.

It let go of the title. It let go of the steady salary. It let go of the benefits. It let go of everything I thought defined me. I knew what I was doing. I was letting go of my fears. I followed my highest level of excitement in micro movements, allowing my heart to do its quiet work. Parallel to living in that excitement, it was chipping away at letting go of the fear. Bit by bit. And when I was finally ready to pull the plug, I had let go of enough that I could fearlessly execute what I needed to do.

Saying to let go is easy. It is the process of letting go that we have to celebrate.

TEACHING MOMENT

It takes energy to hold on to something. Whether it's a belief, a thought, or a brick, there is a certain amount of conscious or unconscious energy spent. For example, the common belief that having a university degree means that you can get a corporate job. If we believe this to be true, then we spend energy enforcing it. We spend energy validating it, we spend energy working on it, we spend energy keeping it alive. But what happens if you let that belief go? Where will the energy go now? That is up to you, if you are aware of it.

If you let go of something, you can allow something else in.

Your fears and pains exist in the parts of you. They do not represent the whole of you. They represent the sliver that has experienced it. They don't define how you show up. They don't define how you choose. They don't define you.

We are made up of many parts. There is a saying how your head argues with your heart, but does it mean the literal heart? No. That's what I mean by parts. The parts you can physically experience and the parts you can't. They all come together to form the whole of you. By being resourceful and whole, it means you tap into the parts that can help. The parts that aren't attached. You are a system—interconnected, complex, and complete.

And when we exist in parts, we can shift in parts. The first is to recognize that we are parts and have different glorious parts within us. And then, we can work on realigning (or letting go) of what no longer serves those parts. This is self-awareness combined with choice.

Beliefs are built up over thousands and thousands of micro moments and learning. For example, the premise that success is defined by how well you do in school has been created and reinforced as a belief since we were children. We are graded. We are rewarded for good grades. We are ranked. We are set in environments designed for competition and comparison. And unless the narrative doesn't change, the beliefs deepen as we begin to live out these truths and validate them with our own experiences.

If beliefs are created in micro moments, then uncreating them is the same. To truly let go of and reconstruct a new belief and narrative, we need to deconstruct and create a new narrative, moment by moment. Next are five tools and techniques to build a mindset where you can deconstruct the beliefs and narratives that no longer serve you, and build new ones. This path you have chosen is not a walk in the park. It takes perseverance, consistency, and discipline to "let go of" old beliefs to make room for new ones. It is the process that is more difficult than the outcomes. But once this mindset exists in you, it will serve you for life. And you will find it is with this mindset that will create the life you want.

FIVE WAYS TO BUILD A "LET IT GO" MINDSET TO DECONSTRUCT A BELIEF AND CREATE A NEW NARRATIVE

"Letting go" is actually a skill. It can be learned. These tools and techniques are small things that you can do to challenge, deconstruct, and rebuild beliefs and new narratives for you to strengthen this muscle. Try them all at different times to create a series of micro moments—like practicing. It is in these small cumulative moments that one day, you will "let go of" those beliefs and narratives that no longer serve you.

1.   IDENTIFY AND FOCUS ON CHANGING THE NARRATIVE IN WHAT YOU CAN CONTROL.

Make two lists. This exercise sets a frame on where to invest your energy.

- One list is "what is within my control."
- The other list is "what is outside of my control."

You want to focus your energy on what you can control first. This is the best use of your energy now.

What is within my control?	What is outside of my control?
Write what you'd like to change that **IS** within your control. Capture all elements including the story, players, feelings, actions, thoughts—everything. For example: I will quit my corporate role. I can control: • Timing, when. • What am I willing to trade off? • Preparations and proposals on how to make this work financially. • My fear pitted against my courage. • How I see and value myself. • My tempo, pace, and quality of my creation (projects).	Write what you'd like to change that **IS NOT** within your control. Capture all elements including the story, players, feelings, actions, thoughts—everything. For example: I will quit my corporate role. I cannot control: • The reaction of my family and friends (especially those who are against the idea). • How my customers will react or receive me. • That people always ask "what do you do" when they first meet me.

2. LOOK FOR EVIDENCE AND CASE STUDIES THAT SUPPORT YOUR NEW NARRATIVE (YES, CONFIRMATION BIAS).

Confirmation bias is the behavior in which you actively seek and acknowledge evidence that supports your hypothesis. For example, when you go for a run and you say "Hello" to everyone, five out of ten respond back. You are a person who makes impact. This also happens when you go out. You say "Good morning" to everyone, and you only count those who say "Good morning" back. You pay attention to the evidence that supports your belief that you are a person who makes an impact.

What is the narrative you want to create now that will serve you better? Write it down and then proactively look for evidence that supports this new narrative.

3. CHALLENGE YOURSELF WITH "BUT WHAT IF THIS WAS NOT TRUE?"

Whatever belief or narrative you tell yourself, pause immediately after the thought and ask yourself "but what if this was not true?" There is nothing you need to do here other than ask this question and reflect on it.

For example:
- I need my corporate job. But what if this was not true? What do I need it for? What do I think I need it for? What evidence suggests that I need it?
- I enjoy sharing with people where I work and what I do. But what if this was not true? What do I need it for?

4. ASK YOURSELF WHY. THEN ASK YOURSELF WHY AGAIN. ASK YOURSELF WHY UNTIL YOU CAN GO NO FURTHER.

This is a reflective internal challenge. You peel back your own anchors and understand deeper your own beliefs to the very root of you. It is important to focus on "why" for yourself. Why is it important to YOU? A tip is to ask yourself why on the first verb that emerges. Below is an example of how you can extract the first **verb** (highlighted in bold) and ask why.

For example: I **need** my corporate job.

Why do I **need** it? So, I can **have** money.
Why do I **want** money? So, I can **provide** my children with a lifestyle of opportunity.
Why is it important that I can **provide**? So, I can **feel good** that I've done all that I can as a mother.
Why is it important that I **feel good**? It is a form of self-**validation**.

Why is it important I **have** validation? I **don't like** failure. I don't like letting myself or others down.
Why **don't I like** failure? It shows my imperfections and something I can't quite accept in myself.

A why thread can go on and on. Stop when you have challenged yourself far enough that it becomes repetitive. From here, you can go back to number 1 and challenge every reply with an alternative truth or ask "what if this were not true?"

5. START WITH LETTING GO OF EASY (OR LITTLE) THINGS FIRST.

It is through practice that you strengthen a muscle. Start by practicing "letting go" of small, everyday things.

For example:

- It is raining and you are annoyed that your hair will get wet. Let it go. Take three breaths and give it no further thought. Move on to the next moment in your life.
- Your colleague made a snide comment of "I'm not sure that's a good idea. I wouldn't do it that way." Let it wash over you. Give it a shrug and let the comments fall to the floor. Move on.
- You feel guilty because you said no to your mother-in-law coming over before dinner. You stayed authentic to

yourself by saying no. Celebrate that. Recognize the guilt. Honor that it exists. Then let it go. You can set it down in a corner for now and come back to it.

As you build the muscle of letting go, this can apply to anything. Fears. Feelings. Thoughts. Perspectives. And as you practice, continuously ask yourself:

How is your relationship now with the thing you want to let go of?

-
-
-

> **YOU CAN NOW GO TO PAGE 242, WHAT ARE YOU LEARNING NOW?**

I WANT TO AVOID

You want to avoid your fears or what causes your fears.

And this is perfectly OK to acknowledge.

There are moments when it's not the right time, capacity, or frame of mind to do anything else. Only you can make this choice on how to move forward, and you do have choice.

You always have choice.

When you think "avoid," what does it mean to you? Write down your understanding of avoid at this moment. To see it, slowly and clearly, is a powerful observation in developing self-awareness.

-
-
-

This is a good start. To understand what avoid means to you.

As you think of your own avoid definition . . .

Which part of you is driving the avoid? Close your eyes and sit with this question. Feel it within you. Which part of you is leading the avoid? It could be physical, mental, emotional, or something else. Feel it.

-

-

-

What makes it important that this part avoids?

-

-

-

This next question is not an easy one. It is an opportunity to take an honest look at yourself and your life. There is always something there, within us, that we can't see just yet. Often, avoidance is associated with pain.

Just sit with this for a bit.

As you observe the part that wants to avoid, what is the pain there that this is avoiding?

-

-

-

Did you discover something? If you did, that's OK. This is the point of the exercise.

If not, that's also OK. If this is the case, you can go to "Five Tips for Avoiding What You Fear."

This is a big moment that you've discovered some pain there. Pain is an important signal that something is not right. It exists so you can pay attention to it and address it. The fear is a protective shell so you don't have to experience the pain again.

Allow these next questions to float within you.

Be gentle and honest with yourself.

What is the pain teaching you?

-
-
-

What would stopping this pain or healing this pain look like for you?

-
-
-

By doing this, what would this allow you to create?

-
-
-

What's a good place to start this?

-
-
-

Thank you for considering this. Thank you for sharing this with yourself. To face your pain and observe it is emotional maturity. It takes courage and strength to get here.

GO TO PAGE 242, WHAT ARE YOU LEARNING NOW?

CASE STUDY

I have a young adult client who spoke to me about her fears. We were brainstorming and having a highly animated conversation on this exact section of my book, and I asked her to give me some real examples from her life that illustrated this concept of fear and pain. She is brilliant in her self-understanding with a clear demonstration of how far she has come in her ability to be self-aware and reflect.

"When I was twelve, I hated going home. I would always get yelled at by my parents. For not doing my homework, for being late, or for reasons that were not so clear to me. So, I would find myself at the mall, or dillydallying on the subway and purposely getting lost. My parents would always call me after school, yelling, 'Where are you? Come home right now!'"

"You would be at the mall or out and about. You didn't want to go home." I replayed back her behaviors. "What would you call that behavior in your own words?"

She laughed. "Avoiding! I was avoiding going home. I didn't want to go home."

We explored this behavior more, identifying characteristics of this avoidance behavior and allowed the client to see the repetition of how this showed up in her life. It was her coded behavior, which allowed her to understand herself better.

"What did this behavior protect you from?" I eventually ventured to ask.

"Getting yelled at constantly. Getting pressured about getting my homework done. But in general, just getting yelled at—but I honestly didn't know why."

It took a few more conversations to unpack her avoidance.

She eventually shared with me, "I really did feel alone when I was twelve. I felt like I was growing up on my own and had to take care of my younger sister. I had a lot of fears, I think. There is this big fear of getting yelled at, which would inevitably happen regardless. But I recognize now that there was pain there for me as a child. The pain underneath was not being loved by my parents."

When she shared this with me, it hit me hard, as her mother.

Now I understood her perspective. I understood her avoidant behavior was connected to a fear, which was connected to a pain. However, while she did choose avoidance at one time in her life, she now chose to overcome and actively rewrite the narrative of the relationship. That is being the architect of her own life.

Author's note: I share this story because of how my own self-awareness has allowed me, as a parent, to show up differently for my child. As a result of this self-awareness, I created choices. And with those choices, I was able to create a different way of interacting and being a parent to my daughter.

With self-awareness, comes choice.

TEACHING MOMENT

Avoidance is natural, safe, and easy. We default to this type of thinking because it is comfortable. Fear is powerful, and there is something worthwhile there for you to explore. And fear doesn't exist by itself. There is always something more beneath the fear or what's causing the fear—and often, it is pain. The fear is simply a shell to protect us from experiencing or addressing the pain. It tells us, stay away, I am keeping you safe. But is safe really living to our fullest potential?

Some will deny there is pain. This is when the pain is too big for them to acknowledge or accept. And then we build walls around them. And the walls become our truths and reality.

For example, passing your hand over a flame hurts. It is painful. You then associate fire with pain and then you fear fire. This is a simple example, but illustrative of physical pain. Can you think of any other associations in your life? All emotions and thoughts of such power are there for us to discover what is useful in it for us. If we can create something like fear that can control us, imagine what it would be like to channel that into something like creating love that can guide us instead.

For example, I've learned that in the pain of being burned, there is a warmth there also. The flame is a place of warmth. I can still pass my hand over the flame, but perhaps much further away. When I do this, I feel warm and cozy, and it doesn't hurt me. I now rather enjoy it.

I invite you to try something new. You can go to page 113, I WANT TO OVERCOME to explore what is possible if we put avoidance aside hypothetically. There are exercises for you to consider an alternative way of using your energy in support of creation instead of avoidance. There may be something there for you.

However, there is always a time, space, capacity, and readiness for which we choose the paths we choose. If you'd like to continue avoiding, here are some tips to support you through this process. Take note of the techniques you have used and how they have been in service to you and then go to page 242, WHAT ARE YOU LEARNING NOW?

FIVE TIPS FOR AVOIDING WHAT YOU FEAR

Avoidance is useful when it's managed. It takes energy to avoid something, so it is important to manage how much energy you are willing to invest in paying attention to your pool of energy and what other parts of your life need that energy.

Here are a few tips you can consider if you choose to avoid your fear.

1. RELAX THROUGH THE EXPERIENCE.

This will help with the mental and physical feelings and thoughts around your fear or what causes your fear. Start with the physical release first. Pay attention to your physical form and begin to take deep breaths, expanding your lungs like a big balloon, in through your nose and out through your mouth. Starting from the top of your head, work your way down to your toes. As you notice the parts of your body, relax those muscles. Relax the muscles in your eyes, blink three times slowly. Release the tension in your jaw, let your tongue settle to the bottom of your mouth. Gently shake your head to soften the neck. Drop your shoulders, loosen your arms. Take a conscious five to seven minutes to do this for yourself.

2. USE HEALTHY DISTRACTIONS.

Healthy distractions allow you to spend your energy on productive activities instead of allowing the fear to be front and center of your life. What activities bring you joy? What activities excite you? What activities allow you to be fully engaged? Running, taking a walk, baking, ironing, cleaning, painting, or reading are some examples. Even napping! These tend to be more physical activities. Unhealthy distractions include alcohol, overworking, snacking on things we know we shouldn't be eating, or pornography.

3. CONNECT WITH A FAITH OR SPIRITUALITY.

If you connect with a faith or religion, you can access something bigger and greater than yourself. Lean into this space and allow it to lead you. Trust your instincts here as it is something that you connect with.

4. LOOK AT THE AVOIDANCE DIRECTLY.

Acknowledge and dissect the avoidance openly. When you can acknowledge it, you can begin to manage it. This is not managing the fear; it is managing the avoidance. At this point, there is an understanding that the fear is there, but to manage it, we avoid it. But do we truly know what that avoid is?

This can sound and feel like:

· How much energy do I want to invest in avoid?
· How will I know how much energy I have invested?
· How much avoid is right for me right now?

5. CONTINUOUSLY CHECK IN ON YOUR AVOID CHOICE.

Everything changes all the time. As you live and experience your life, you change (whether you want to or not). You are constantly integrating your experiences and learning from them (whether you are aware or not). As such, check in on whether your avoid choice continues to serve you in managing your fear in your life at the moment. You can seek the support of friends to talk through it or seek professionals such as therapists or counseling. You can also self-reflect through these questions:

- What is my avoid in service to now?
- If avoid wasn't an option right now, what would I choose instead?
- Go through to page 113, I WANT TO OVERCOME or page 124, I WANT TO REFRAME scenarios for fun. Was it difficult or easy? Why?

AFTER EACH TOOL, TAKE A MOMENT TO GO TO PAGE 242, WHAT ARE YOU LEARNING NOW? THIS WILL HELP YOU ANCHOR WHAT YOU'RE OBSERVING ABOUT YOURSELF WITH THE TOOLS.

I HAVE NOT EXPERIENCED WHAT MAKES THIS FEAR, A FEAR

You have a fear. You recognize and acknowledge it.

You see "what makes this fear, a fear." It's why the fear exists.

You also recognize and acknowledge that you have not experienced "what makes this fear, a fear" before.

This is good work. It's hard work to get this far. It truly is.

This is super interesting, though. Take your time with the next few questions. Reread it if you need to. Go slowly. They are meant to be thought-provoking and is supposed to allow you to explore new and different parts of yourself. Write them down so you can see yourself.

Great . . . let's look at what we have on the table.

You have a fear.

On the one hand, you see what makes this fear, a fear.

And yet, you have not experienced what makes this fear, a fear before.

This is interesting. Pause here to observe that in yourself.

Go slow. Reread the question again if it doesn't land for you. Reread it out loud if it helps.

What would you have to . . . believe is true . . . about never having experienced this "what makes my fear, a fear" to feel this fear?

Since you've never experienced this "what makes my fear, a fear," what would you have to . . . believe is true . . . to feel this fear?

As you answer this, start each belief with, "I believe that . . ."

-
-
-

Take a moment to reflect on your reply. Take a moment to observe yourself.

What makes this TRUE a limiting belief? These are unconscious and personal biases we hold against ourselves. Sometimes, it's hard to recognize and see them for what they are. Beliefs that limit. They limit growth. They limit potential. They limit joy. They limit living.

At this moment, there is a fear. There is what makes this fear a fear. However, what makes this fear a fear lives outside of you. You have not experienced this before. This is illustrated in Figure 7. As shown, there is some belief that is created within you as a result of what makes this fear a fear that feeds your fear. It is this belief that is called a limiting belief.

At this point, you can stand outside of yourself and observe all these in parts. This is exactly where you want to be when you are observing yourself. Detached and in control. This is good to practice.

Figure 7: What would you have to believe is true about never having experienced this "what makes my fear, a fear" to feel this fear?

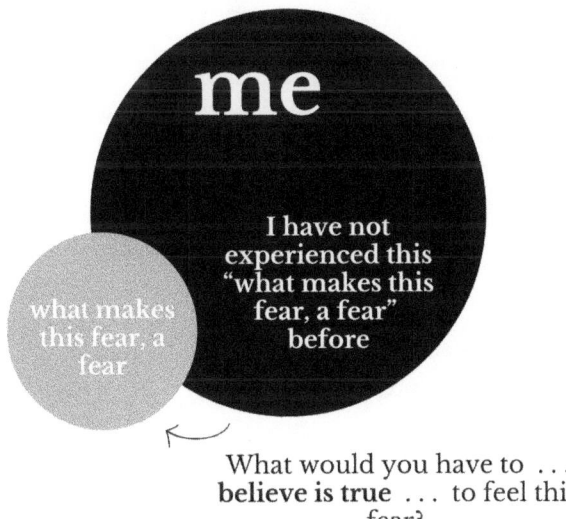

me

I have not experienced this "what makes this fear, a fear" before

what makes this fear, a fear

What would you have to ... **believe is true** ... to feel this fear?

Let's keep exploring this now that you're able to be an observer to yourself.

In this next question, really pause and be true to your answer. Feel it's authenticity within you. This is important to do. You are answering for your true self, not what you think you should answer.

For this limiting belief . . .

Is this limiting belief still serving you right now?

-
-
-

If you answered no, you're ready to challenge your limiting belief and build a new belief that will serve you. Go to page 159, NO, THIS LIMITING BELIEF IS NOT SERVING ME NOW.

If you answered yes, it is about discovering what keeps this belief alive. It is important that you celebrate your acknowledgment, but also recognize that you grow and develop at a pace that is authentic to you. Go to page 164, YES, THIS LIMITING BELIEF IS STILL SERVING ME NOW.

CASE STUDY

A child, who loves to sing, is singing joyously at home in the kitchen. However, at that time, a parent is working from home and about to jump on to a conference call and is frazzled with work and snaps at the child, "Stop singing. I have a headache! It's making it worse. Why are you so noisy?"

The child stops in her tracks. Quiet. She is processing her parent's response. "Can I just sing quietly?"

The agitated parent shakes their head, "No, I said to be quiet. I need you to be quiet. I am going to have a meeting now!"

The child's older sibling, who happened to be in the living room nearby, laughs. "Your singing is so awful," they scoff, "it sounds like a piano out of tune!"

This pattern repeats. Every time the child starts to sing, especially in the kitchen or near the working parent, the parent snaps at the child that she is too noisy and is disturbing them.

The older sibling has also become a regular contributor, saying things like "You sound like a dying bird again!" every time the child breaks into song.

Over time, the child begins to believe that they are disturbing others when they sing and that they sing badly. As this continues to be reinforced, the belief deepens and eventually becomes this child's truth.

"Whether you believe you can do a thing or not, you are right." –Henry Ford

TEACHING MOMENT

Limiting beliefs are exactly that—a belief within us, that limits us. They are stories that we hold as truths and subconsciously live in. They are formed from external inputs we have in our lives such as culture, society, expectations, media, or parenting experiences. They shape how we see the world, and more importantly, how we see ourselves. They shape the decisions we make. They shape how we interact with other people. The key characteristic about limiting beliefs is that they hold us back.

The truth is that we have unlimited potential with unlimited possibilities.

When we believe that this is true, we can tap into our true and full potential, allowing us to live the life we want. In this way of thinking, we are limitless.

Only you can agree to what you accept is true about yourself.

NO, THIS LIMITING BELIEF IS NOT SERVING ME NOW

This is a big moment.

The energy that you are carrying now and the conscious understanding that this limiting belief is NOT serving you now is a very important moment.

You are now in control.

Say the words in your mind . . .

"This limiting belief is NOT serving me now."

"I am in control."

You can now rewrite your own narrative and alter whatever belief is holding you back. You are the master of your life. You are the author of your story.

Take a moment to rewrite all of this. It is in this creation of possibilities that you can explore your full potential.

What about this belief is NOT serving you NOW?

-
-
-

What belief would serve you now instead?

-
-
-

How would this new belief serve you now?

-
-
-

What will allow this belief to turn into your truth?

-
-
-

Well done. Now that you know how to challenge your limiting beliefs, you can continuously come back to visit this tool.

As we begin to wrap this up, go to page 242, WHAT ARE YOU LEARNING NOW?

TEACHING MOMENT

It takes a lot of courage to challenge a belief. The thing with beliefs is that we accepted and agreed to this belief as part of who we are. So naturally, when we challenge it, we question ourselves, we feel bad, we feel guilt, we doubt.

Nothing affects you until you agree to be affected.

When you can step into your own power and know and feel you are in control, everything changes. To challenge limiting beliefs means that you can "return to sender." That's exactly what you are doing. The sender could be your parents, teachers, peers, the media, or society. It could be a combination of them. It does not matter. The only thing that matters is that you have the choice to send it back.

CASE STUDY

Here are some of my limiting beliefs that I have actively challenged. The limiting belief from childhood that I needed straight A's to be a good child. The limiting belief that was passed through a generational lens that I had to get a degree to be considered successful. The limiting belief that I learned in school, such as farting is something to be ashamed of. I honestly have no control of my flatulence.

The average person flatulates eight to fourteen times per day! Why is it embarrassing then? Even for adults!

In this, I share a personal story about challenging my own limiting beliefs and how this has significantly changed how I relate to my children. I am considered Generation X. My parents are baby boomers and first-generation immigrants. They worked hard to earn degrees in their home country and moved to Canada to build better lives for their family. They worked steady "9 to 5" jobs for decades, bought a home, and invested in the standard retirement savings plans and pensions. When they retired, they were considered "lifers," meaning that they worked their whole career at one company until retirement. They were upper-middle class. They could afford to send their three daughters to all sorts of activities, have once a year big vacations, and retire comfortably. That was the formula to life. I grew up with this understanding of how my life should be. The belief was that I needed a degree to be considered successful. If you didn't get into university, you were considered a failure. This is the story that I also told my two daughters—until this year (at the time of writing, in the year 2024). My eldest was in grade 12 and most students at this age were applying to universities, but she didn't really seem that interested in going. She challenged the value of a degree. She saw how my work shifted from corporate to content creator and entrepreneur. She saw the joy that it brought me. She saw the freedom. She was experiencing a different kind of mom.

I was no longer the "tiger mom" that I used to be. I let go

of what people thought and worked on what "we" thought was best for us as partners—as mother and daughter. We explored philosophy and perspective. We challenged each other's limiting beliefs and iterated definitions over and over. We looked at cultures and human operating models. We read *Sapiens: A Brief History of Humankind* by Yuval Noah Harari as part of our mother-daughter book club and discussed concepts in the book. And finally, we talked extensively about the benefits of having a degree, but also the trade-offs. We tabled consequences, opportunities, and options. In the end, as part of her consideration for university entry, she applied with one criterion, which university had the best international networking and global opportunities? Nothing else mattered. In fact, her only goal for university at the time was to build her personal network, be involved in global issues through student bodies and volunteering, and grow her personal projects. And even if she didn't go to university, I was OK with that and loved her all the same. No pressure. No expectations. All our limiting beliefs around education and success were challenged and reframed, and it allowed our relationship to flourish beyond ways I never expected. It was truly life changing, for all of us.

You are complete as you are. Return everything that doesn't belong to you, to sender.

YES, THIS LIMITING BELIEF IS STILL SERVING ME NOW

This is a great recognition up to this point.

Recognizing a limiting belief is not easy. Acknowledging that there is something still there for you is also a very courageous thing to see.

Do not judge yourself.

If you feel an emotion, let it wash over you. Feel it for what it is, but let it pass, including judgment. Let it pass.

At the end, we need to be authentic and true to ourselves. We owe ourselves that.

This limiting belief . . .

Write it down. Capture it. Say it out loud.

Take your time with this next question.

What makes it important that you continue to keep this limiting belief alive?

-
-
-

Remember, don't judge your response. There's something there you need to see, feel, and experience. This is why these questions exist. Allow you to see yourself fully and truly.

We also understand that a limiting belief is something that is gifted to us. Well, there comes a moment that its lifetime usage has run out and we outgrow it, especially as you grow and create the life you want.

How will you know this limiting belief has ended its service to you?

•

•

•

Oh, it is so beautiful that you're able to think through this very important question and allow yourself to better understand your own limiting belief. You may have multiple limiting beliefs; you can come back to this exercise as many times as it serves you. The important thing is not the answer itself, that's secondary. The key is to recognize that the limiting belief has a time limit. While you may not have the exact answer right now to the above question, at least you've put in some thought. Continue to iterate this answer because it will change.

If this limiting belief is continuing to serve you, go to page 242, WHAT ARE YOU LEARNING NOW?

If this limiting belief is truly not serving you and you'd like to challenge it, go to page 159, NO, THIS LIMITING BELIEF IS NOT SERVING ME NOW.

Now that you know, you know, and you can't unknow it. The question is . . . what now?

CASE STUDY

I wanted to leave my corporate role for at least five years before I actually acted on it. I had a lot of limiting beliefs during that time that served me up until I finally did quit. Limiting beliefs have lifespans. Until you dismantle the limiting belief from within, you will discover that it will continue to serve you.

One such limiting belief is the belief that I am defined by my career. How do I answer, "What do you do?" This question inevitably comes up any time I meet someone new, especially in a professional setting. To challenge this, I changed my LinkedIn header with a personal mission statement and stopped using my title. I started introducing myself differently, encompassing all the personas that I carried, not just my work one. I introduced myself as a coach. I introduced myself as "The Chinese Soup Lady." And I saw how it opened a whole new world of interest and dialogue. People were genuinely interested in my passion projects and who I was. The interest in my corporate job scaled back, and I could engage people in the things that I loved. It was at this point I understood that this limiting belief no longer served me. My career did not define who I was.

Another such belief was that I would not be viewed the same on the outside world without my title and organization. How would people see me if they didn't recognize the name of the organization that I put on my name tag at conferences? Would people still approach me? Would I still be able to sit on the various advisory boards I was already on? This limiting belief died quite suddenly and accidentally. During such a conference held by my undergraduate university, the organization had pulled the title and organization of my one-person coaching business rather than my full-time role. They couldn't reprint in time, so I was stuck with it. But I discovered that no one really cared! They were more interested in discussing the topics the conference was exploring around AI. It was at this point I understood that this limiting belief no longer served me. People were more interested in what I had to say as an individual around shared interests than what I did at work and who I worked for.

The biggest limiting belief in keeping my corporate job was that I needed it to survive financially. I believed that this was my one and only source of income. It was easy. It was stable. It was predictable. This belief was challenged when I discovered that I could run a side coaching business, a coaching school business, and a content creation business parallel to my full-time job. I was intentional to test this limiting belief at the cost of personal time and resources.

I wanted to know what the trade-offs were. I wanted to know if it was possible to offset income in different ways. I discovered that this belief of income through a corporate role (especially one that I was no longer passionate about) no longer served me when I had alternatives. The death of this limiting belief was one of the big contributors to my corporate resignation. And up until today, I have rewritten my narrative around the "doing what you love" and income relationship. It has given me new perspective on living in possibilities and new understanding and appreciation of the journeys we are all on in our lives.

TEACHING MOMENT

The important lesson of identifying a limiting belief is that it has a limited lifespan of service to us, if you so choose. It can almost be comical in the logical sense that if we know it's a limiting belief, why do we continue to carry it? Some limiting beliefs exist for a reason. It is in understanding ourselves fully that we can see why they serve us at a particular time, and to continuously evaluate whether it still serves us or not. In this light, if we begin to understand ourselves more deeply, we can grow and learn through this understanding to make more informed choices about how we show up and how we want to live our lives. There is no right or wrong choice. There is simply an understanding and acceptance in why that choice exists and what we can learn from it.

There also exists a spectrum of believing. It starts with truth to us on one end and eventually becomes a limiting belief as we challenge what we think is truth inside us and whether what we believe is in service to us or not. There will always be moments of doubt and fluctuations along this path, especially if we lean toward external validation (like asking input from peers or colleagues). This is very normal and very human. First, habits are hard to break, and thinking habits are no different. Second, external validation is equally hard to break because the stories we hear have been told to us for so long, we don't think any other story could exist.

Look within yourself about what you want to create for your life and what's in the way. More often than not, there are many limiting beliefs in the way.

Let's say, hypothetically for a moment, that you take one belief that exists for you right now that is in the way of something you desire. There are two possibilities here for this belief.

There is a possibility that this is a limiting belief.

Let's assume that this belief is NOT serving you right now. The thinking may sound like this: "What would it be like for me if this belief didn't exist?" Let's play with this new way of thinking. It's hypothetical anyway, right?

You can go to page 159, NO, THIS LIMITING BELIEF IS NOT SERVING ME NOW.

There is also the possibility that this is a genuine belief, and there is something useful for you.

Let's assume this is true. The thinking may sound like this: "How can I take this belief and turn it into something useful?" Something useful is very personal and unique to you. This could be a lesson, a way of being, a new thought, a way of feeling, an action, a dream, a way of showing up, anything. There is always this perspective available.

I AM STUCK

Being stuck is a temporary experience.

LEARNING OBJECTIVES OF THIS TOOL:

- Develop self-awareness in your own definitions of stuck.
- Learn how to create an anchor and direct your energy.
- Understand what parts of yourself you need to confront to move forward.

If you haven't read the section LET'S BEGIN! start with that to get grounded first.

You are stuck.

This is not always an easy place to be in.

It is amazing that you recognize you are stuck.

The great thing about being stuck is that even if it doesn't feel like it, stuck is a temporary experience.

Stuck often means you know where you'd like to go from here in a general sense. It may not be perfect, but it's directional. This is different from lost. If you don't have a direction, then you are lost and go to page 181, I AM LOST.

As we explore this stuck, allow whatever comes to mind to surface. You can write it down or draw it out so that you can see it.

Allow whatever parts come to your mind to surface as well. If it's the first thing that comes to your mind, let it. Take a few moments to feel yourself and all the parts available. They won't all surface at once. In fact, some parts that surface may surprise you. And these parts can have whatever label you feel it represents. It could be an emotion, a thought, a physical part, a value, a belief, a thing . . . you don't need to worry about labeling it properly. Only you know what it means.

Let's explore this stuck.

This stuck that exists in the present you. The you right now.

As you think of this stuck, if you were to be unstuck . . .

What does unstuck look like for you?

-
-
-

This is great! Your unstuck exists.

This is your anchor.

It is a desire in you. It is what you want. It is where you want to be. This is important to capture. It will be your true north for the remainder of the session. Your energy goes where your focus goes.

What would this anchor allow for you?

-
-
-

As you look at this anchor . . .

Which parts of you are already leaning forward? A part is how you define it. It can be physical, spiritual, mental, or something else. The key is to know that it is a part of you. It is a part that you recognize. It is a part you can define.

-
-
-

Which parts are not?

-
-
-

Can you see the parts of yourself that are leaning in and the parts that aren't?

For example, when the heart really wants something, but the head is holding back. This often happens in a career situation or even in relationships. You want to do something you're passionate about, but it doesn't pay the bills. You love them, but culturally, they don't fit the mold.

Another example is, when you start a side business and would like to be unstuck in having more time to work on it. Your hands and head are committed, they are ready to work, but the body is constantly tired. It doesn't have the capacity to do more.

Referencing Figure 8, there are parts that lean in (parts that aren't stuck) and parts that lean out (parts that are stuck). As you move toward fulfilling your anchor, there needs to be alignment in you as a whole person. It doesn't mean that the parts that are leaning out need to lean in completely, but they do need to be "confronted" to be unstuck.

Figure 8: Confronting the parts of you that aren't going forward

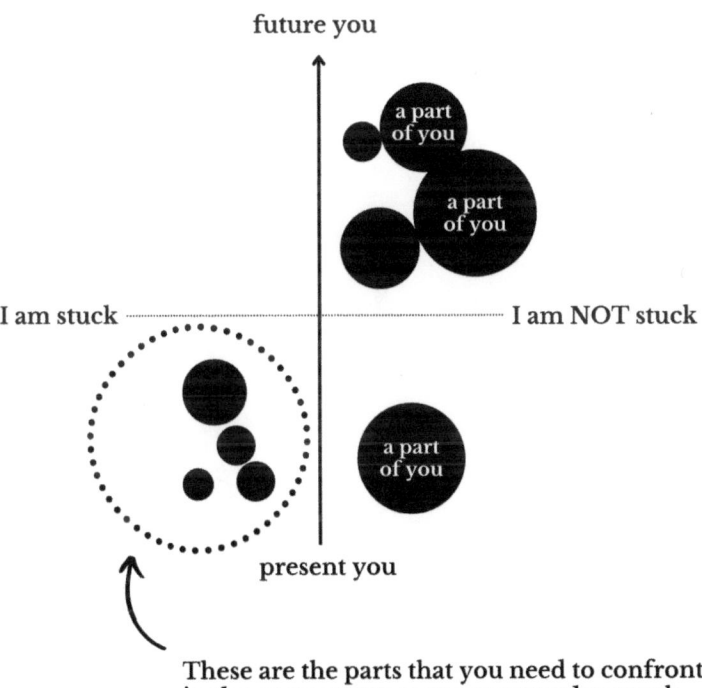

These are the parts that you need to confront in the present you to move toward unstuck.

It is fascinating to observe yourself in parts. This is very powerful. You can now see the parts of you that you may need to confront to allow you to be unstuck.

As you look at these parts that aren't leaning in . . .

What in these parts aren't allowing you to lean in?

-
-
-

What do you need to let go of or allow in yourself for these parts to lean in?

-
-
-

What would you say to these parts to enable that?

-
-
-

> THIS IS A GOOD TIME TO GO TO PAGE 242,
> WHAT ARE YOU LEARNING NOW?

CASE STUDY

This is a beautiful story about confronting the parts that aren't serving us right now.

"I want to connect more with my mother," Judith replied when I asked her what she would like to explore in our coaching session. "She lives in the US, while I live in Hong Kong. My sister in the UK calls and visits her more often than I do."

We explored what connecting more with her mother meant. She had all the right answers. She knew she should call more regularly. She knew she could send a quick hello message whenever she wanted to. She knew she could set up a regular weekly or biweekly "touch base" through the calendar. She knew what she needed to do, and yet, she couldn't.

She was stuck.

"You actually know what you need to do," I said. "Which part of you knows this and wants to do this?"

"My head," she said, laughing. "It's probably something I could google, like, 'how to stay in touch with long-distance parents.'"

"And which part of you is not leaning into this right now?" I asked.

She paused and frowned. "I think my heart. My heart isn't really there right now to do it. I always find something else more important to do. I mean, I know, sending a text is not hard, but . . . honestly, I just don't feel like doing it."

"I hear two things. The first is that it can be easy to do. The second is that it's your heart that doesn't feel like doing it."

She nodded.

"What positive impact does this bring your heart, by not doing it?"

This pause was much longer.

"It feels . . . hmmm . . . it feels . . ." She took in one deep breath and sighed. "It feels . . . justified."

I allowed some time before I mirrored it back to her. "It feels . . . justified," I simply repeated very slowly.

She nodded again.

"Share with me, what do you mean by justified?" I asked, equally slowly, holding pace.

"Well, my mom never calls me," she answered, her tone slightly agitated. "Even my sister never calls me. So, I always asked myself, why should I take the first step? Why should I be the only one putting in effort to maintain these relationships?"

This is where she was stuck.

We unpacked more of the tension between the parts of her leaning in and the parts that were not. This allowed her to see the different parts of herself and understand what was holding it back.

In the end, Judith realized that her heart, in this moment, was not in a loving position. It was hurt and protective and wanted to equalize the playing field, but her head knew that it wasn't the right thing to do. She concluded that she would step up to the plate first and make those calls first and propose a regular touch base and see where that would take her. In this, she confronted her hurt heart. She didn't try to heal it; she simply offered it a conditional perspective to "try and see where it goes."

TEACHING MOMENT

Being stuck is a great place to be in! It means that a destination already exists.

The only thing in the way is that you don't know how to move forward. There exists a clarity in you in knowing where you want to be. The approach of this tool is to step beyond solutioning logically. Again, there is nothing here to solve, yet. Coaching takes a perspective that you are whole, complete, and resourceful, and it is using this lens that this tool works within the whole of you, as a person. The tool is designed to evaluate and understand the different parts within you, knowing that there is a whole. It is the parts that we explore, allowing you to understand yourself slowly, in parts. This is the layered approach in this tool.

We often lump ourselves as one entity and stay stuck, thinking we have failed ourselves as a whole. However, that is usually not the case. It is only a part of us that is blocked.

For example, the most common New Year's resolution is to stay healthy. The part called the brain has a plan (and it's magically convinced the heart to join it starting January 1). It will buy a gym membership, it will stop drinking coffee, it will cut out sweets, and it will cook at home more often. However, come February 1, the heart begins to lose motivation and takes over the body. The body goes back to its comfortable routine before January 1, and you are OK with it. However, the head still knows what it needs to do to stay healthy, but both the heart and the body aren't listening. We know what we need to do, but we can't. Why is this? Which part has tapped out? And more importantly, why? What needs to be confronted to stay true to what we want as a whole person?

As you understand your parts, you can dissect what exists within them. What makes this part lean in? What makes another part lean out? What are the parts that are in conflict within us that we need to address? Which part is more important, and why? Once you see all the parts of yourself in the situation and understand what they represent, you can confront those parts to be in full alignment to work toward your anchor.

We are composed of so many little parts that make us whole.

I AM LOST

It is not about getting from point 1 to point 2. It is about getting from point 1 to point 1.01 first.

LEARNING OBJECTIVES OF THIS TOOL:

- Expand your understanding of lost and break it up into parts.
- Differentiate between stuck and lost.
- Create a visual map of lost and its parts.
- Discover your desired experience with these lost parts.
- Choose how you want to spend your energy moving forward.

If you haven't read the section LET'S BEGIN! start with that to get grounded first.

You are lost.

That is a very powerful statement. Nicely done for saying this out loud in your consciousness. Not many people can acknowledge this position and admit to not knowing where they are. It is certainly not comfortable to be lost. Choosing this statement as something to work on is very empowering.

You are lost.

What is lost? Where is lost?

Use the blank worksheet provided or a blank piece of paper for this self-coaching session. It will help you capture key points and support the visualization exercise. You can also download a template of this worksheet from the QR code at the back of the book.

PART 1: DEFINE THE CONTEXT OF LOST TO YOURSELF

Write down your answers. What is this lost? Which part of your life? Which part of you? Your answers are your own. There is no right or wrong way to experience lost.

Start with, "I am lost in my . . ."

-
-
-

PART 2: EXTRACT THE PARTS OF THE STORY

Write down key words found in your context. For this session, these are called parts.

Coach's note: If you answered, "I would like to be not lost," try again or stay here. You may be lost.

For example, being lost at looking for your next career role may have parts such as the new role, your existing or old role, happiness, passion, money, location, urgency.

Or being lost at relationships may have parts such as me, desired partner, historical partners, memories, expectations, feelings, loneliness.

Look at your story. Look at its parts.

To be not lost, what would you like to have instead?

Start your reflection with "I would like to . . ."

-
-
-

If you've got an answer, you may not be as lost as you think. You may just be stuck. The answer represents an end position.

If you don't have an end position, then you are lost. Stuck means that you know where you'd like to go from here in a general sense. It may not be perfect, but it's directional. This is different from lost. If you've answered the above question, go to page 171, I AM STUCK.

PART 3: VISUALIZATION EXERCISE

This next part is a visualization exercise. You can use a separate blank page or the worksheet attached. There is an example on page 188.

READY?

1. Draw yourself in the middle of the page.
2. Draw the parts that you extracted from your lost story as one circle per part. Two things to keep in mind:
   a. The bigger the circle, the more important that part is to you.
   b. The further away the circle is to you, the more lost that part is to you.
3. Draw a line from you to each circle. This is the experience you are having with that part.
4. For each line, express what you would like to have happen with this circle. Start with "I would like to . . ." Take your time with this. Feel it.

Now, take a few moments to reflect on these questions with your map from Part 3.

Notice ...

Which one is the biggest circle? This is the most important one to you now.

Which one is the closest circle? This is the one that is the most NOT lost.

Are the circles complementary or conflicting?

Are the circles pulling you in the same or different directions?

What you have now created is a prioritized list of desired end states. These are all the statements starting with "I would like to ..."

What are you learning about your lost now?

-
-
-

How does this map now inform you on where you would like to invest your energy going forward?

-
-
-

This is good work. In such a short time, you were able to construct a perspective that can function as a map! This is a very useful skill to have. The ability to visualize and extrapolate yourself out in parts is important to create possibilities. This is what it means to step outside of yourself. This is increasing and practicing self-awareness.

**NOW IS A GOOD TIME TO GO TO PAGE 242,
WHAT ARE YOU LEARNING NOW?**

CASE STUDY

This is my own lost context when I quit my corporate role.

PART 1: DEFINE THE CONTEXT OF LOST

I am lost in my life right now. There is a lot going on internally and externally to me. While I have a lot of projects and thinking, I am pulled in so many directions because I like to be busy. I am lost in how to focus my energy. It is too much.

PART 2: EXTRACT THE PARTS OF THE STORY

- Corporate role
- My purpose
- Self-healing
- Income
- Who am I?
- Stability

PART 3: VISUALIZATION EXERCISE

Figure 9: Case study of "I am lost"

Context: I am lost in my life right now. There is a lot going on internally and externally to me. While I have a lot of projects and thinking, I am pulled in so many directions because I like to be busy. I am lost in how to focus my energy. It is too much.

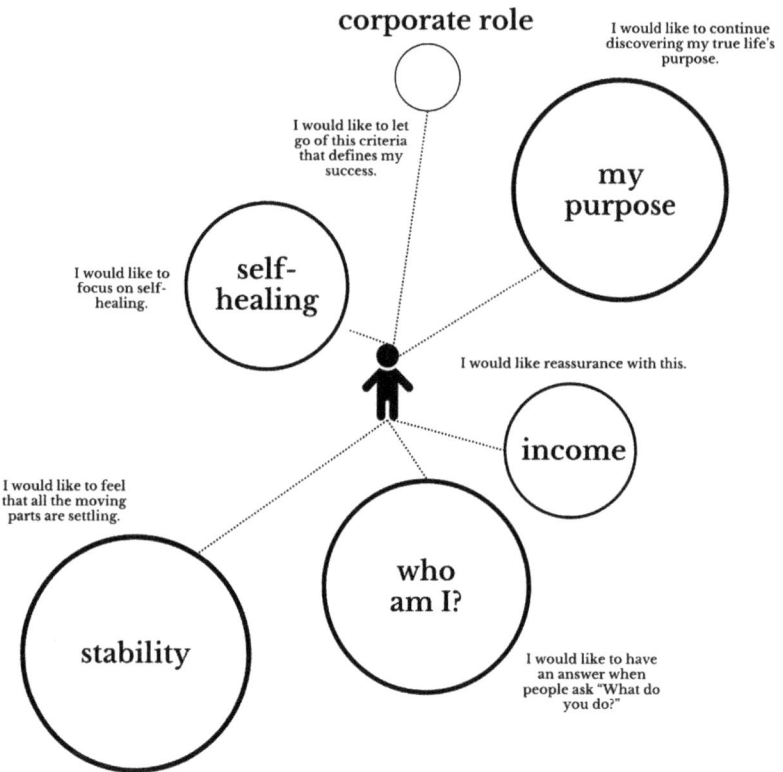

Reflection question: What are you learning about your lost now?

My lost is a combination of so many things. I didn't realize how many parts there are to this lost. However, I am not as lost as I thought I was. It felt like everything was pulling me in all directions, but these key things are contributing to my feeling of lost. Anything not shown here is managed, which I feel good about. I will further break down stability for more clarity since it's the most important and the furthest away from me right now.

Reflection question: How does this map now inform you on where you would like to invest your energy going forward?

Stability and finding my purpose are where I will focus my energy a little more going forward. The other parts are holding for now since I have more clarity on them. For my purpose, I have a plan for this. The problem is that I am investing too much energy here, doing too much. To have more clarity in stability, I will shift some energy into this space over the next week and see where I land.

This was a helpful exercise for me to see myself in moments of lost. It is an exercise of thought organization. By breaking up my lost into parts, I can see what my lost is composed of. By understanding my experience of each part, I know where I want to go with that part. By seeing all my desires, I can choose and move my life forward meaningfully with intention.

TEACHING MOMENT

Lost is a relative position. You may feel lost at that moment, but are you really lost? Zoom out and break it up in parts and you will discover that you are not really lost. There will always be points of references, both where you are and where you would like to be. With the right tools and thinking space, you will ultimately find yourself again.

We default to comfort when we experience unfamiliar or unknown territory. To lean into this space requires conscious and intentional energy. So, when we perceive we are lost, we freeze. We don't have enough to move forward. We don't have enough to know where we are going. Whether it's information or courage or something else, we do not like "not knowing." We are risk-adverse creatures. We default to comfort knowing there is more for us.

As outcome-focused human beings, we see journeys as from point 1 to point 2. Point 2 is what we want. Point 2 is our end desire. If we have point 2, we will be fulfilled, content, and achieved. But what about point 1.01? What about point 1.02? What do these intermittent little points offer us? Self-awareness allows for us to continuously evaluate what we define as progress or lost. It evaluates our current perspective and asks if it continues to serve us in what we think is our point 2. Lost is a half-empty perspective. Even if we are at point 1.5 and we feel lost, we forget the celebration of being halfway there. The visual map that is created with your lost context and its parts will change. It will change as you live your life. The size of the circles will change. The relationships you have with these circles will change. Even the circles may change. This visual map is a living perspective. It is useful to take stock of it every so often and check in to ensure our intentions are still aligned with where we want to go.

Being lost is just a relative position. Are you really lost?

I AM LOST
(WORKING PAGE 1)

You can use this space for your guided coaching session for page 181, I AM LOST. You can also download a template of this worksheet from the QR code at the back of the book.

Part 1: Define lost in context to your life or to yourself. Write down your answers. Start with "I am lost in my . . ."

Part 2: Write down key words found in your context (called parts).

I AM LOST
(WORKING PAGE 2)

PART 3: PUTTING IT ALL TOGETHER ON A MAP

1. Draw yourself in the middle of the page.

2. Draw the parts that you extracted from your lost story, one circle per part. Two things to keep in mind:
    a. The bigger the circle, the more important that part is to you.
    b. The further away the circle is to you, the more lost that part is to you.

3. Draw a line from you to each circle. This is the experience you are having with that part.

4. For each line, express what you would like to have happen with this circle. Start with "I would like to . . ." Take your time with this. Feel it.

I DON'T KNOW

LEARNING OBJECTIVES OF THIS TOOL:

- Expand your understanding of I don't know.
- Identify how big your I don't know is.
- Learn to break up I don't know into parts.
- Learn visualization techniques to increase reflective and creative thinking.
- Zoom out of your I don't know into a higher perspective to see what you do know.

If you haven't read the section LET'S BEGIN! start with that to get grounded first.

You don't know.

Out of all the statements available, it is not easy to select this one. As human beings, we think we know, and we want to know.

To recognize that you are in a place of "I don't know" is a very powerful position.

To start, it is OK to not know.

"I don't know" is a very common experience for many people. They just don't admit it.

We will work through this slowly, as with all exploratory experiences in this book.

So, let's begin . . .

Take three deep measured breaths by inhaling slowly and allowing yourself three counts before you exhale slowly and repeat this two more times.

Now, as you think about this "I don't know" . . .

How big is it relative to yourself?

-
-
-

There is no right or wrong answer here. This is your current experience of your "I don't know."

Which statements connect with you more?

1. My "I don't know" is about the same size as me.

    - I feel grounded.
    - I am not drowning.
    - Let's go to page 212, I DON'T KNOW ABOUT I DON'T KNOW.

2. My "I don't know" is so much bigger than me.

    - I feel overwhelmed.
    - I am drowning.
    - Let's go to page 201, I DON'T KNOW IS BIGGER THAN ME.

3. I still don't know.

    - Let's go to page 212, I DON'T KNOW ABOUT I DON'T KNOW.

CASE STUDY

Miranda was a client I had for a demo session I was doing for my students. She was a friend of a friend who wanted to experience professional coaching and was willing to give it a try in front of a live audience. She was a professional marketer in Asia who was at the pinnacle of her career, and she was curious to explore what she could do next professionally. She was well spoken and articulate, but her responses were guarded with one-word answers such as "maybe" or "perhaps."

"When you say maybe, what does maybe mean?" I asked very slowly.

She paused and looked up. "Maybe means I'm not sure," she answered very matter-of-factly.

I chose stillness at this point. The pause, as a technique, has so much power. It allows the human mind to continue searching because sometimes the logical mind is uncomfortable with pauses.

"It means I don't know . . ." she continued after some time when I didn't respond.

At this point, for me as a teacher, there were two routes I could have taken. One route would be to continue the silence and create a large awkward moment for the client in front of a live audience. It would be a battle of who could stay silent longer. Given that my client had already deferred to answer the question twice, I didn't want to take this route and make the space unsafe for her. The second route was to go back to previous material and work in a space that the client was familiar and comfortable with. This meant taking a few steps back.

"Let's go back to what you were looking for," I said. "At the beginning, I heard two things. One is that you love your career. And the second is that you feel there is something more."

"Yes," she confirmed.

"And when I asked what is that more, I heard the word 'missing.' That something was missing." I'm quite paced here, allowing the client into a reflective space again. I then asked my next question very slowly, pausing in between each word, "What can you tell me about what you know is NOT missing?"

"What is NOT missing?" she repeated.

"Yes, what can you tell me about what you know is NOT missing?" I repeated the question. This question is a double negative. It gives pause to the mind because it catches the mind off guard. This type of question also allows the client to table what is positive in an otherwise thought-to-be negative situation.

She paused in thought. "Well, I love my job, still. The drive to succeed is still there, and I get a lot of satisfaction from it. I'm still challenged and enjoy my colleagues very much."

"How wonderful, Miranda! I hear there are many beautiful things that bring you joy and what is NOT missing right now. You have a love of your job. You have a love of the challenges. You have an enjoyment of your colleagues. I also heard you say the word "still" three times. Is that part of NOT missing?"

She nodded. "Yes, this is true . . ."

This allowed me to play back to her a new frame of reference. What she could do next professionally had a foundation. It was a foundation that included knowing she still loved her work, the challenges, and her colleagues.

This helped her move away from "I don't know" so that we could continue a productive conversation.

TEACHING MOMENT

I don't know is only scary when it's a big unknown blob. Start with what you do know.

Let's start with the definition of knowing.

To know, a verb, is a state of being aware or informed. This can also include being in possession of knowledge, information, or intelligence. When you say "I don't know," it is not that you know NOTHING. This is a surety. The reflective tools in this section are designed to allow you to work through a process of elimination based on what you do know, which is an important starting point. As illustrated in Figure 10, from a search perspective, it is important to recognize that you are NOT starting with NOTHING. Knowing that you don't know is already knowing SOMETHING. This is called being at the seat of yourself. To be able to stand outside of yourself and see how you are thinking is a very important step to self-awareness. If you can shift to this state, to look at yourself and see how you are experiencing this moment, the reflective tools become so much more powerful and this NOT KNOWING slowly evolves to narrowing down in a direction of KNOWING. We begin to build out a picture of what you KNOW based on what you

DO NOT KNOW. This will set a base for a boundary so this I DON'T KNOW begins to take shape rather than feel like a vast black hole.

Figure 10: Shaping "I don't know" into what you know

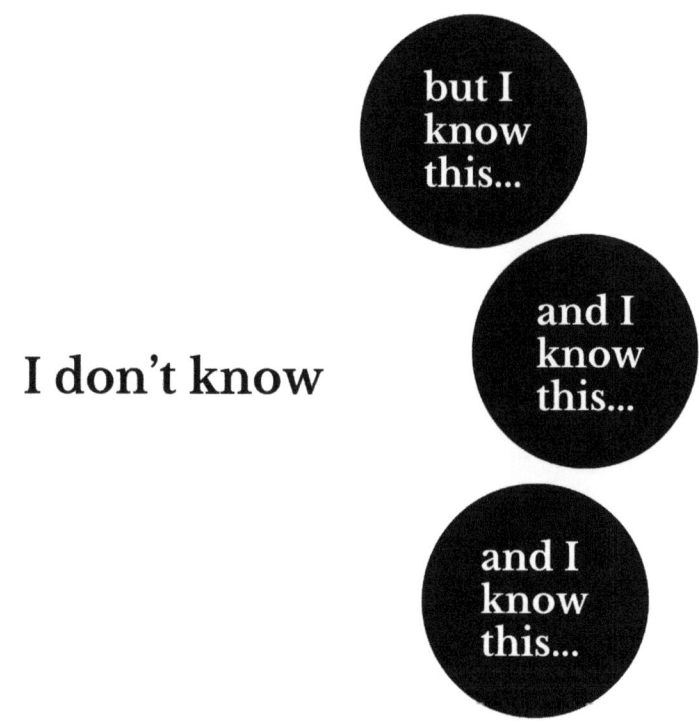

I DON'T KNOW IS BIGGER THAN ME

You may be thinking . . .

"How did I get here?"
"Why am I here?"
"Where do I start?"
"How do I begin?"

These are common questions when we feel like we are not in control.

This is big for you right now. Yes, it is big. It is very big.

This is not an easy experience to be in. This feeling of being overwhelmed. This feeling of drowning.

Let's slow things down a bit.

Take one deep measured breath by inhaling slowly and allowing yourself three counts before you exhale slowly. Repeat this two more times.

Well done for acknowledging that this is bigger than you. It is brave — it is strong — to recognize it for what it is.

For this next piece, close your eyes to visualize what emerges from the next question when you are ready.

As you do, practice the slow measured breathing you just did earlier as you visualize it and capture this on paper as words or drawings. You can use the worksheet labeled "I don't know is bigger than me" (working page). You can also download a template of this worksheet from the QR code at the back of the book.

Whatever emerges, it is important that you can see it. This is a key part to this tool. Whatever emerges, allow it to emerge fully, whether it's a feeling, a thought, a perspective, or a way of being.

Ready? Don't forget to close your eyes and breathe. Take as long as you need.

-
-
-

When we say big . . . what . . . is . . . this . . . big?
Can you describe it?

-
-
-

Well done for giving this "big" shape and form on paper. The amazing thing is that you can contain it on a piece of paper.

You can take it outside of you. You can see it now. You can observe it outside of you. It sits there . . . It just sits there.

Take a few moments to look at it. Hold it out in front of you.

And as you observe your "big," consider this . . .

-
-
-

What would "breaking it up" look like?

Name the broken-up parts on paper. You can use the worksheet labeled "I don't know is bigger than me (working page), Part 2" to support you through this. There's no right or wrong way in "breaking it up." You slice it as you like. They can be parts of the big, they can be feelings, they can be thoughts.

-
-
-

What makes it important to you to break it up this way?

-
-
-

What do you know about each of these smaller parts?

-
-
-

How do you see your "I don't know" now?

-
-
-

Think about the experience that just happened when you answered the earlier questions.

What inside you allowed you to break it from "big" to "smaller" parts?

-
-
-

How has your statement of "I don't know is bigger than me" changed now that you can see it in pieces?

-
-
-

What will this allow you now?

-
-
-

**NOW IS A GREAT MOMENT TO GO TO PAGE 242,
WHAT ARE YOU LEARNING NOW?**

CASE STUDY

I had a client who came to me almost every week drowning. There was always something—new and big—overwhelming him. He was constantly drowning and never seemed to have a moment of reprise.

It started with work. This is a common theme for a lot of the executives I work with.

I've added my narrative as a coach in italics.

Coach: I hear there is a lot going on. Tell me more.

Client: So, you know all the challenges I've been having at work since our last conversation. And that hasn't died down. In fact, it's gotten bigger. You also know my mom was recently diagnosed with cancer, and since I am the only child, it's primarily fallen on me to step in. My dad is in no state to do anything, and I want him to focus on his own health. This week, my wife got sick. The children's activities continued, and I had to carry a lot of the household. It was hard.

Coach: That is a lot.

I paused. This allows the client to continue releasing whatever is needed should he require it. He nods.

What would you like to have instead?

Client: I don't know . . . There's so much.

Coach: Imagine a hammer. Aim it at this "I don't know." Break it up. What are those pieces?

This is a reflective question with no direction or guidance on how the client should break it up.

Client:	Well, the first piece I see is to stop feeling so manic and crazy. Like I am running around all the time. I don't even have time for myself to breathe.
Coach:	I hear first, find a sense of calm for yourself. Go on . . .
Client:	And then to support my wife and ensure she's in good health. I think that's important. She's my partner, and without her, it just made things worse! I didn't realize it until this week. I am going nuts.
Coach:	Yes, I hear it is important to you to have your partner back.
Client:	Yes . . . and then everything else, I can figure out. I mean, it's really a matter of prioritizing after that. I think I can manage after that. I mean, it's just work, which, when I think about it, is just work. And my mom's cancer will still be there for the next few weeks, so . . . I think it's really just getting to a state of calm and having my partner in crime back.
Coach:	Nice. I see three parts to what you'd like to have. One. Be in a calm space for yourself first. Two. Get your partner back. And three, then strategize the best way forward. Is that right?
Client:	Yes.
Coach:	I appreciate these three key parts of your I don't know. What makes it important that you broke them up this way?
	Questions of importance allows the expression of values. This is what is important to them.
Client:	I think it's what can bring me peace. Without it, I feel like a chicken running around with its head cut off. I can't make any rational decision. I can't think or function properly. I'm not even sure I can show up as a good boss to my team or even a good father to my children.

Coach: Wow. You want to show up as best as you can. This is why its important to find calm and peace first, because this will allow you to manage everything else.

Client: Oh, yes. Yes. Yes, I want to find my inner calm.

By breaking up the client's situation into pieces, he was able to see it in parts. What started out as a big unmanageable mess, turned into a prioritized list. He understood what was important and why.

TEACHING MOMENT

A situation that is too big and overwhelming feels like a drowning experience. The water level is too high. In this state, the mind and body are focused on one thing: Seek safety. There is no room for prioritization, processing, or feeling anything else. There is no room for breathing. This is how an "I don't know" that is too big shows up. It is impossible to ask a drowning victim what they would like to have or what they need when they are drowning and can't breathe. They seek safety first. Physical safety above all else. The intention of the tool is not to resolve or fix anything. It is to create a safe space when the experience is too overwhelming. It is to stabilize the experience first. Stabilizing is also progress. This is illustrated in Figure 11. Shifting from a state of drowning to not drowning is as much progress and a call for celebration as shifting to a state of thriving.

Figure 11: You don't always need to see thriving to celebrate progress

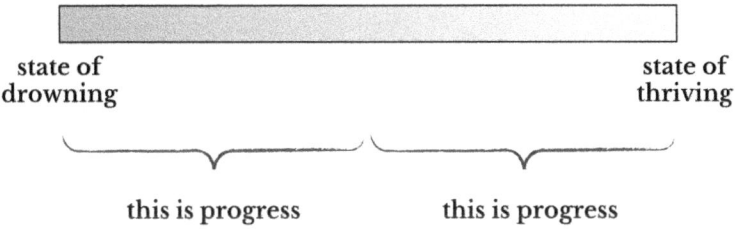

With this, you can practice creating a self-sustainable stabilizing capability from within.

When something feels too big, break it up.

Understand why it is broken up the way it is. It is not the parts that matter, but the discovery of what matters most. In this lens, we understand and learn where and how to focus our precious energy in service to the life we want.

I DON'T KNOW IS BIGGER THAN ME
(WORKING PAGE)

You can use this space for your guided coaching session for page 201, I DON'T KNOW IS BIGGER THAN ME. You can also download a template of this worksheet from the QR code at the back of the book.

PART 1: CLOSE YOUR EYES TO VISUALIZE WHAT EMERGES FROM THIS QUESTION. **WHEN YOU SAY BIG . . . WHAT . . . IS . . . THIS . . . BIG? CAN YOU DESCRIBE IT?**

PART 2: WHAT WOULD BREAKING UP YOUR BIG "I DON'T KNOW" LOOK LIKE? NAME THE PARTS IN THE TABLE BELOW.

You can also download a template of this worksheet from the QR code at the back of the book.

The parts of your big "I don't know"	What do you know about this part?

I DON'T KNOW ABOUT I DON'T KNOW

Recognizing that you don't know about not knowing is a great place to start. There is a willingness there because you are here.

It almost feels circular, doesn't it?

So, let's explore this.

Take three deep breaths and work through these questions slowly. Intentionally slow down so you can step outside of yourself to see what and how you're experiencing yourself.

Use the blank worksheet provided to you or a blank piece of paper for this self-coaching session. It will help you capture key points and support the visualization exercise. You can also download a template of this worksheet from the QR code at the back of the book.

PART 1: DEFINE "I DON'T KNOW"

Write down your answers. What is this "I don't know?" Which part of your life? Which part of you? Your answers are your own. There is no right or wrong way to experience "I don't know."

Start with "I don't know about [insert context]." Add as many details as you need.

PART 2: VISUALIZATION EXERCISE

This next part is a visualization exercise. You can use a separate blank page or the worksheet attached. There is an example on page 217. You can close your eyes for this exercise to help with visualization.

Allow whatever emerges to show up, as it is, raw and unprocessed. And if you can't answer the question, reset, take a few breaths, and try again. This may take some practice to do, so don't be discouraged if nothing comes to mind right away.

Picture yourself standing in a field. It can be a field of flowers, wheat, grass, balloons, or whatever connects with you. But it is a field. A big field. A field so big, in fact, that you don't know where you are.

This is you.

Deep in "I don't know."

This field is your [insert context], what do you see now? Describe it.

-
-
-

What does this represent for you?

-
-
-

What do you know about this?

-
-
-

Now imagine that you are standing outside of yourself from above. You can see yourself down there. A little speck in this giant field. How amazing!

Slowly zoom out.

Like as if it were a screen of sorts. You can pinch it with your fingers.

You can zoom out quite far.

And as you zoom out, you begin to see more. You can see so much of the characteristics of the landscape in which this field sits. You can see yourself, as a little speck, standing in the middle of your field of [insert context].

Keep zooming out.

You can see things. You can see so much more than you originally did standing in the middle of the field.

These things are where you want to go. These things in your story. Things you want.

What do you see now?

-
-
-

Seeing this, where do you want to go?

-
-
-

What makes it important that you head toward that direction?

-
-
-

What do you know now with this map about [insert context]?

-
-
-

IF YOU CAME FROM "I CAN'T DO IT," GO BACK
TO WHERE YOU LEFT OFF AT PAGE 224, I CAN'T
DO IT.

IF NOT, NOW IS A GOOD TIME TO GO TO PAGE
242, WHAT ARE YOU LEARNING NOW?

CASE STUDY

I had a client who did not know how to move forward from a career perspective. He was unemployed and looking for work. It was a tough job market out there. He had a lot of ideas on things to explore and where to start.

We did the field reflection. *I've added my narrative as a coach in italics.*

Coach: You're in this field. This field is the career part of your life. You are lost in it. What do you see?

Client: The grass is tall and it's like wheat. I can't really see anything. It's pretty tall, actually. And the grass sways, but it's pretty dense. It's so dense, I can't really see beyond a few feet in front of me, and there's no clear marked path.

Coach: Oh wow. Tall wheat grass all around you with no visible way out.

Client: Yeah . . . something like that. *He chuckled.*

Coach: Tell me what the grass represents?

I am curious how he sees himself relative to his situation. This will allow him to see himself relative to his experience.

Client: I guess the confusion of ideas and thoughts. There are too many, and I keep applying to jobs, hundreds over the last few weeks, with almost no response. That's part of the grass too. I feel like I am doing so much and yet yielding nothing. I am busy, every day. Thinking, applying, brainstorming, but I can't go anywhere. There's no progress.

Coach:	Yes, I can see how dense it is in there, all jammed. And yet, stuck.
	OK, now imagine you're looking at this scene on a screen.
	You see yourself in this yellow wheat field. Zoom out a little bit.
	What do you see?
Client:	I see myself as a dot. And everything around it is yellow. A lot of yellow wheat everywhere.
Coach:	This is good. I also hear you want to go somewhere.
Client:	Yes! I want to move! Even if it's one step out of that crazy field. It's frustrating.
Coach:	Moving is a great intention. *I focus on what's positive and possible.*
	Share with me, what does moving mean to you?
Client:	Like, be able to make some progress somewhere. Slowly make my way out of this field. Maybe get to a place that's not so dense and crowded. It's too busy for me. I can't see anything.
Coach:	What's stopping you from moving?
Client:	\<Long pause\>

Here the client goes into a reflective thinking space. The answer is not readily accessible so the pause allows his mind to search beyond a logical answer.

Huh. I guess I am too consumed that I am surrounded. I didn't really try to push my way forward in one direction. I guess I am a bit greedy and trying to go in all directions.

Analogies are excellent tools in creating different frames in the mind. When you have multiple frames in your mind, different perspectives emerge and with that, options. This is the power of creation. Frames and perspectives are infinite. The ability to create these perspectives exist within you. You are resourceful in this light, and with this, you can create whatever you want.

TEACHING MOMENT

This approach is similar to the "I am lost" tool. It explores the "I don't know" from a reflective perspective through visualization. "I don't know" becomes tangible beyond a black void (which is usually how "I don't know" feels). It allows the reflective and creative mind to step forward from the more dominant logical and rational mind. This is an important state to tap into for deeper self-awareness and self-discovery. Visualization is one common tool employed in coaching to expand the mind. If "I don't know" continues to exist, try any one of the next five visualization techniques to step away from your logical mind.

FIVE VISUALIZATION PROMPTS TO SHIFT YOUR THINKING FROM LOGICAL TO REFLECTIVE CREATION

1. USE COLORS.

Use colors to describe it. It could be in the context of a feeling, a situation, a person. Play with the concept of how your experience shows up in colors. What color is it? What makes it that color? Are there multiple colors? Do they blend? What color would you like it to be?

2. THINK CANDY!

Consider your experience in candies. If you went into a candy store, what candy is it? Can you describe this candy? What do the candies represent? Describe the candy store. How are the candies organized (or not)? Who else is there in the store? There is a lot you can explore in both the itemized candies and the candy store itself.

3. USE TEXTURES.

If you could take it out and feel it, what texture would it
be? What makes it this texture? How does it feel to you?
What do you think of it? How do you feel about it? What
do you want to do with it? How will this texture serve or
not serve you now?

4. DROP YOURSELF INTO A FIELD.

Visualize yourself in a field. What surrounds the field?
What can you see? What can you not see? Now zoom out.
Pinch your mind with two fingers as if it were a screen.
Zoom far out. Describe it. Are there any points of reference? Where would you like to be? How do you feel about
being there? What would you like to do now? What happens next? What's in the way?

5. TAKE IT OUT OF YOU.

Reach into yourself and take it out of you. Pull out that
feeling, thought, idea, instinct, or whatever it is that is
part of your experience. It sits in your hand. You can see it.
What does it look like? What does it feel like in your hand?
What makes it the way it is? What inside you created it?
What would you like to do with it now?

After each visualization exercise, take a moment to go to page 242, WHAT ARE YOU LEARNING NOW? This will help you anchor what you're observing about yourself with the tools.

I DON'T KNOW ABOUT
I DON'T KNOW
(WORKING PAGE)

You can use this space for your guided coaching session for page 212, I DON'T KNOW ABOUT I DON'T KNOW.

You can also download a template of this worksheet from the QR code at the back of the book.

PART 1: DEFINE "I DON'T KNOW"

Define "I don't know" in context to your life or to yourself. Write down your answers. What is this "I don't know?" Which part of your life? Which part of you? Your answers are your own. There is no right or wrong way to experience "I don't know."

PART 2: VISUALIZATION EXERCISE

This blank space is for you to use for your field visualization exercise. This field is your [insert context]. Draw yourself, draw what you see, draw where you want to go.

I CAN'T DO IT

To challenge "I can't do it" is taking full responsibility for your life.

LEARNING OBJECTIVE OF THIS TOOL:

- Expand your understanding of "I can't do it."
- Learn to flip and challenge your perspectives.

If you haven't read the section LET'S BEGIN! start with that to get grounded first.

"I can't do it."

This is why you're here.

It is because this statement resonates with you at this moment.

That is a big statement.

Start by acknowledging the "I" part of this statement. **I** means **YOU**. It means taking ownership for yourself. It means taking accountability for where you are right now. It means stepping forward to claim what is yours. There is power in this position because you are in control.

Next, acknowledge the "DO IT" part of this statement. To do something means you have a desire. You have intention. You have something that you want. You are here to explore possibilities and work toward living the life you want.

And when you combine "I" and "DO IT," it creates a powerful accountability statement with intention. Look at what you have right now and explore all the possibilities of creation with this.

I _____ DO IT.

The only word in the way right now is "CAN'T."

And when you break down "CAN'T," it becomes "CAN NOT." The definition of "CAN" is defined as "to be able to." So, the only word in the way right now is "NOT."

Take a pause here. Reflect on this.

You are here because of these four words. Of which only one of these words is what stands in the way between you and your DO IT.

For these questions, you can use a piece of paper and write it down or draw whatever comes to mind or record it. Find a way to observe what is showing up for you through the question.

When you think about this "NOT" that exists in your statement . . .

What is this NOT?

-
-
-

For this next question, read it slowly. Start your answer with "I would like . . ."

What would you like to have instead of this NOT?

"I would like . . ."

-
-
-

And with your "what you would like . . ." what will allow this NOT to NOT EXIST in this situation?

Write it down. Create at least ten responses. This is not to say that the NOT does not exist at all, but for it to not exist in regard to your "would like" . . .

The question again is . . .

What will allow this NOT to NOT EXIST in this situation?

-
-
-

IF YOU'RE STILL DRAWING A BLANK ON THE ABOVE ANSWER, GO TO PAGE 212, I DON'T KNOW ABOUT I DON'T KNOW TO EXPLORE THIS NOT KNOWING.

IF YOUR PAGE IS NOT BLANK, THIS IS A GREAT TIME TO GO TO PAGE 242, WHAT ARE YOU LEARNING NOW?

***

If you're coming back from page 212, I DON'T KNOW ABOUT I DON'T KNOW, continue here.

Look at what you captured about what you don't know and what you know now.

How can this knowing allow your NOT to NOT EXIST in your situation?

-
-
-

Well done.

**THIS IS A GREAT TIME TO GO TO PAGE 242,
WHAT ARE YOU LEARNING NOW?**

CASE STUDY

I teach a flip technique to a lot of my clients. It is particularly interesting when I teach it to middle management executives. This technique allows them to lean into the role of being a coach instead of being a manager to their teams. There is a perception that new managers must manage, direct, and tell. They must fix things, rather than ask and guide and allow their teams to fix their problems themselves.

These clients come to me with challenges that their teams bring to them. They will tell me that their teams complain about:

"There's too much work, and some of the deadlines, I can't meet. I've already told Team A that I need more time. I honestly think there is a buffer because they don't need to get this to Team B until end of next week. They keep telling me they need to review it ahead of time, but how much review do they really need?"

"There are issues between us and the audit team. They want us to document everything. We've already sent them the emails as part of the process, but they want more. What do we do?"

"I'm having some trouble with Marty. I don't think he understands what I need right now. Is there any way you can speak to his boss?"

I hear their stories and acknowledge their situations. As new managers, they have their own set of working challenges as individual contributors, and now they must take on the challenges of their teams too. It can feel like a lot to carry.

"I want you to try something next time a team member comes to you," I suggested. "I want you to acknowledge your team member, thank them for sharing, and then slowly ask this question: What would you like to have instead? This is the flip question." I teach them pacing, I get them to practice it a few times, and I coach them to pay attention to the responses. I would suggest follow-up questions such as "And what would allow you to fulfill that?" or "What's the best way for you to move forward on that?"

During our next sessions, I will always ask how it went. And the responses are all the same.

"It's allowed my team member to table their own desires and figure it out themselves. It wasn't about me fixing it for them or giving them the answers. To be honest, I sometimes don't have answers."

"I love how this turns the tables back to the team member. I know they tell me these things so that I can help them in some way, but this technique allows them to come up with their own solutions. I appreciate how I'm asking them for their own critical thinking around their own problems. I feel it allows me to show up better as a manager because I'm not taking on everyone's problems now."

"It works! I just have to be patient to allow them to answer, but you're right about pacing. It has to be slow enough so that they can come up with their own answers. I love it. I use this on my kids and husband now."

The question flips perspectives. It allows the team members to shift from frames of "can't do" to "can do." It creates possibilities and sets a platform for the manager to guide their team member forward.

TEACHING MOMENT

This technique is called a flip. A flip is when a perspective shifts. When you come into the perspective of "I can't do it," it is a frame of loss. It is something that you do not have; in this case, it's the ability to do something. This is when you are looking at your situation as a half-empty glass. The question "What would you like to have instead?" creates a frame of gain. It creates the ability to look at something you can have, achieve, or be. This is when you look at your situation as a half-full glass. The situation remains the same, but the lens in which you are looking at your situation has shifted toward something that is possible and in line with what you truly want.

There are many ways to "flip" a perspective. Question-based prompts that challenge perspective can enable a flip in self-coaching. This is intentional and allows for increased self-awareness. Flips can happen across any spectrums that have opposite positions.

For example, flipping from positions of:
- loss to gain (as previously used) and vice versa
- external to internal, such as from other people to the self

- time, such as now to future
- states, such as emotional to physical
- all other spectrums where human beings can experi-ence their situation.

The power is in recognizing that you have the ability and capability to flip. You are not bound by one perspective. You are not limited. You can create possibilities. And once you can do that, you have choice.

With perspectives, comes choices.

I HAVE DISMANTLED I CAN'T DO IT

Reflect on what you've just discovered within yourself.

This is amazing that you have found something! No matter how small, big, or what shape, size, or form it comes in.

It is the start of beginning to understand that what fuels this is WITHIN YOU. It is another part of your "I CAN'T DO IT" that we are now dismantling. The "NOT" now has an element that is within your control. This is because it is something created from inside of you that fuels this "NOT." And you can control this fuel. Let us call this "NOT" "What's in the way?"

There is no right or wrong to what you discover within. And each time you come back to this exercise, you will discover something new. What may surprise you is discovering what fuels this "what's in the way" may be in parts, or belongs to different parts of you, or show up in ways that you didn't expect.

Take a closer look at this "what's in the way" element . . .

Can you take it out and hold it in your hand? Try and visualize it.

-
-
-

Capture your observations on paper if it's helpful. Thoughts, shapes, feelings, emotions, perspectives, or colors. Capture it all. Allow them to take shape and form so you can see what's within yourself. This is your mirror.

Now that you can see this "what's in the way" . . . in your hand . . .

What, within you, keeps this "what's in the way" alive? There is something there from inside you that pushes fuel up your arm, to your hand, and keeps it burning.

What, within you, fuels it?

-
-
-

Is something there?
Can you feel it?
Can you see it?

What does it feel like?

-
-
-

What needs to be true, in you, to **slow** or **stop** fueling this?

-

-

-

NOW, GO TO PAGE 242, WHAT ARE YOU
LEARNING NOW?

CASE STUDY

Liz came to me overwhelmed and crying with one big theme that stood out loud and clear as we started our coaching session.

"I can't do it!" she exclaimed. "I just can't do it!"

I allowed her to cry it out, supporting the safe space so she could experience all her emotions in that moment.

"What do you mean, you can't do it?" I gently asked.

"I have so much going on in my life! I have so much work on my plate. I've got a business trip coming up and some big project deliverables. I even have three more calls tonight with Asia that I need to attend. I've got my mom who is going through procedures. And then to top it all off, my husband has been busy with his own things, so I feel like a lot of the children's activities and planning have shifted back to me. We've been eating takeout all week, and I usually cook or make soup for the family. And I missed my daughter's ballet recital last weekend because I had to work. Lisa, I can't do this anymore! I can't!" She rattled off her list of things to do quickly, counting them on her fingers as she went.

I paused, allowing the moment to settle. But more importantly, allowing the pace of the conversation to slow. This is important in coaching moments. This will allow the client's mind to slow as well. Very often, a client will mirror the pace of the coach, so in fact, any one of us can control the pace of a conversation if you are intentional in how you pace your words.

"Wow, Liz," I started, intentionally slower, "your plate looks like it is overflowing."

She nodded slowly, and I noticed she took one deep breath, which allowed her breathing to slow overall. These are important observations that a coach can make during a conversation and, if needed, can mirror this back to the client and ask what is happening within the client.

We continued to expand the different items on her plate, until I found this interesting nugget that surfaced.

"It's not that I don't want to do all these things," she started. "I love everything I do now, it's just happening all at once."

"Yes, there is certainly a lot on your plate right now." I gave her a giant smile as she nodded.

"You . . . love . . . everything . . . you . . . do," I echoed slowly, emphasizing the word "everything."

She continued to nod.

"And as you love everything you do, the plate is over-crowded. What would you like to see happen here?" I asked, slowing again.

She sighed and her shoulders relaxed visibly. "I'd like some breathing space. I just want some space to get things organized so it doesn't feel like everything is flying at me left, right, and center. I just want some breathing room."

We explored what this meant for her and expanded on both what "breathing space" looked and felt like. This allowed her to visualize and talk through strategies she was comfortable to implement, which included letting go of some of the items for now such as cooking and being OK with ordering takeout for her family.

"I hear you've got some great ideas on how to manage your plate over the next few weeks," I recapped after she shared some of her learning. "I want to circle back to your original statement of I CAN'T DO IT. What are your thoughts now about I CAN'T DO IT?"

She laughed, giving me her usual bright smile. "I guess I can do it, but just not all at once."

I nodded. "So, you can do it, just not all at the same time."

"Right," she added and threw out some ideas about what she could do to create more balance in her life and put some things on pause or delegate out.

We ended the session with Liz feeling lighter not because she really couldn't do it, but because she couldn't do it all right now. We challenged her "I can't do it" perspective and reframed it to "I can do it, just not all right now."

TEACHING MOMENT

The phrase "I can't do it" is structured in the lens of DOING. The outcome is tangible, as is defined by the word DO IT, with IT being the outcome. This is where we most often get stuck in our thinking. When this phrase is used, there is an attempt to solution something and fix it. This is a natural and rational way humans behave. There is no wrong or right in this approach. It is only one way to look at "I can't do it."

Coaching is not about solutioning. If it were, we could take a consulting approach and draw out some beautiful PESTLE or SWOT models and be done with it. Coaching is not solutioning or consulting. Coaching is a learning experience that will ultimately allow you to get to where you'd like to be and what you want—and usually in the unlikeliest of ways. It is about accessing perspectives. It is about seeing, creating, and living in possibilities and potential.

We can't solve problems by using the same kind of thinking we used when we created them.

There are a lot of gain-framed elements in the statement of "I can't do it." We've dissected this earlier as you worked through the "I can't do it" tool. It is important to acknowledge these because this begins to steer the mind away from a loss frame and toward possibilities. It is far easier to launch forward when you realize that you've taken most of the steps already. This is how to counter negativity bias, which is the behavior that human beings tend to give more weight to negative characteristics than positive ones.

The idea here is to flush out the positive characteristics of "I can't do it" to illustrate how many gain frames there are. Consider Figure 12 that separates the difference in loss (half-empty) and gain (half-full) positions in the "I can't do it" statement.

Figure 12: The loss and gain positions of each word in the phrase "I can't do it"

I = taking accountability

do = to execute, to complete, to achieve, there is intention!

it = there's a goal!

can = this possibility exists

not = this is what's in the way

gain positions | loss positions

Out of the five words, there is only one negatively positioned word (or loss frame), which is the NOT. Individually, all the other words on their own can hold a positive position. The NOT negates any of the gain elements and creates one big loss experience.

FIVE WAYS TO REFRAME AN "I CAN'T DO IT" PERSPECTIVE

To reframe your perspective means to have an alternative way to see the statement "I can't do it." It creates a set of different possibilities in how to see your situation, allowing you choice in how you want to create what you want.

1. **ADD THE WORD "YET" TO THE END OF ANY NEGATIVELY FRAMED PERSPECTIVE.**

    One word can change the whole position of the sentence.

    I can't do it = I can't do it, yet.
    I can't find it = I can't find it, yet.
    I'm not there = I'm not there, yet.

    From here, consider what will allow you to build the bridge between now and yet.

2. **LABEL EVERYTHING AS AN EXCUSE.**

    Whatever reason you have to justify why you can't do it, label it as an excuse. Tell yourself, "That's just an excuse…" This will challenge how you see your perspective, and now allow yourself to accept or settle with this position.

3. REMOVE THE "NOT" AND ANY NEGATIVE POSITIONS.

Literally remove the NOT (or any negative words) from the statement. Write it down like that. Say it to yourself like that. Repeat it to yourself like that. What you say, what you repeat to yourself becomes what you think. And what you think becomes truth. There is power behind changing the narrative as words.

4. BUILD A CASE FOR WHY YOU CAN DO IT.

If you can convince yourself that you can't do it, you can convince yourself that you can do it. Build a case, looking for evidence and support, that you can do it.

5. FIND YOUR CHEERLEADERS.

Sometimes it is difficult to see past our own biases and arguments. In these cases, seek external support. Find your cheerleaders. These are the encouraging and supportive people who can give you the new narrative you need to reframe your "I can't do it."

WHAT ARE YOU LEARNING NOW?

Well done that you have gotten this far in the process!

There is no right or wrong way to go about this.
There is no right or wrong way to think.
There are no right or wrong outcomes.

Coaching is a learning experience. And only you can answer what you are learning and how it applies to your life.

It is important to celebrate THIS moment of allowing yourself to be here, right now. With yourself.

Take your time to go through these learning moments. Allow it to come through, whatever emerges as it is.

You don't need to process it or analyze it. You simply need to let it emerge as it is.

Think back about what you've just experienced . . .

What's emerging for you now?

-
-
-

Take a few minutes to sit with it and observe it.

Is it a thought?
Is it a feeling?
Is it a way of being?
Is it an image?

If you can, capture it on paper, in whatever form it shows up.

And finally . . .

What are you learning now?
Up to this point.

Right now.

-
-
-

What are you learning about yourself?

-

-

-

IF YOU'VE COME FROM "I CAN'T DO IT," GO TO PAGE 233, I HAVE DISMANTLED I CAN'T DO IT OR PAGE 250, WHAT WILL YOU DO WITH THIS LEARNING NOW?

You can always come back to the teaching moment later.

CASE STUDY

I had a client who was getting back into the corporate workforce after deciding to step away from being a full-time stay-at-home mom and spoke passionately about her new role in helping students at a local university as a career counselor. She spoke of visions for being an inspiring leader for these students.

"What defines a leader?" I asked her.

"Oh, someone with a title who actually manages and leads people. They have a team," she replied matter-of-factly.

I nodded. "What defines an inspiring leader?"

This gave her pause. "Someone who can inspire the team to follow them. Someone who mobilizes people naturally, and people are drawn to them. Someone you look up to. Someone you want to follow."

"I love that." I smiled at her. I made a mental note to go back to all her definitions. This is important for the client to clearly see all her definitions on the table. This is the mirroring effect so she can observe herself. "So, an inspiring leader mobilizes, draws people in to follow them."

She nodded.

"I'm curious . . ." I paused and slowed down my pace as I asked the question to allow her to further explore her understanding of an inspiring leader. "What allows a leader to mobilize and draw people in to follow them?"

She didn't answer right away. The question was designed to be more challenging because it required deeper reflection of her understanding of the definition of an inspiring leader. "Well, they have charisma, and they don't force people to do something but create a story that allows their teams to believe what they are doing is worthy and impactful. I think they put out a mission that people can connect with."

Her answers were data for me to work with. I loved it! I got excited about this type of data because I had so many definitions of how she saw a leader that I could begin to allow her to see all of it as well. "I love this, Amy! A charming, mission-led individual is an inspiring leader."

She nodded quickly, smiling at me.

"You originally said they had to have at title and lead a team," I said. I could see her smile soften now. "Does a charming mission-led person need these to be an inspiring leader?"

Now she frowned. I was curious about this frown. This is the power of observation. Do you notice how I did not make any deductions or assumptions about this behavior? I was simply curious about it. I mentally took another note about this and filed it away. I had no expectations for where her answer would go.

"Um . . ." She hesitated and gave me a sheepish smile with a shrug. "No, I guess not?"

She ended her answer with a slightly higher inflection tone. Was it a question? Another observation that I noted in my mind. At this point, I let the frown go because as coach, I am working with data in the moment. "Was that a question?" I asked gently.

"Hmmm, yes . . . because I am not sure," she admitted.

The client was experiencing a challenge of her limiting beliefs. I allowed her to see the conflicting definitions of inspiring leader that emerged from herself. We played with this disconnect in understanding for a few more rounds of questions and answers.

"What's emerging for you now?" I asked.

"Huh, I guess you don't have to have a title or lead a team or be CEO to be an inspiring leader," she concluded. "I guess anyone can have a vision or anyone can be charismatic and informally lead a group."

I smiled. "That's amazing! Wow, anyone can be an inspiring leader!"

She returned my smile. "Yes, yes!"

"What are you learning now?" I asked.

"That I can be an inspiring leader!"

This is where we eventually ended up.

Learning is a key tenet of coaching. It is not my job to come to conclusions of what Amy should or should not learn. It is hers. It is her job to make meaning out of what was emerging for her.

TEACHING MOMENT

As human beings, we are constantly learning. This has been our gift from inception, even as a fetus inside our mother's womb, we are learning languages before we are born. We are learning whether we choose to or not, so the questions are: Do you care? And how conscious are you of this learning?

The definition of reflection is to give something "serious thought or consideration." This doesn't necessarily include learning, which is why as part of the coaching process, learning is an important and integral element of coaching. While reflections and observations are useful, learning in coaching is the process of taking what you observe from yourself and intentionally putting your own meaning and your own understanding to it. It is recreating definitions or perspectives based on what you're experiencing now. It is discovering something you didn't know before. It can be any or all of these at any moment of your self-coaching experience. The key part of this process is that it is intentional, and it usually happens toward the end of a coaching moment.

Learning can be in any shape or form. Learning can show up as anything. We are trained in our education system to answer logically when a teacher asks, "What have you learned?" Who defines what is right or wrong learning in a coaching conversation? Who is the coaching conversation in service to?

Here are some examples of learnings:

- I've learned to go easy on myself. This is a new way of being.
- I've learned I need to plan better. This is an improved way of doing.
- I've learned about my limiting beliefs. This is a new way of thinking.
- I've learned I think too much. This offers a choice in how to show up.
- I've learned to question my definitions. This is to think about thinking.
- I've learned I'm not ready. This is a perspective on current position.
- I've learned nothing. Go to page 194 to further explore this statement. This is an interesting one.

Learning is a part of discovery. When you give intentional voice, shape, or form to your learning, it is powerful. You can be intentional in using it. This application is the integration of the learning and of you toward a new you. This is the experience of growth.

WHAT WILL YOU DO WITH THIS LEARNING NOW?

Look at what you've captured as learning.

This is marvelous! Well done! This is the gift to yourself, these learnings, insights, and new perspectives — whatever they are to you. It can even be a new feeling or a seed of thought. New doesn't need to be shiny or big. You define your own new. You define your own learning.

And with this learning . . .

Let's go back to the statement that you started with at the beginning of this session.

What was it?

-
-
-

What will you do with this learning now?

-
-
-

Based on the opening statement of your session, how will this serve you going forward?

-
-
-

AND FINALLY, YOU CAN NOW MOVE TO PAGE 256 TO CLOSE THE SESSION: WRAPPING UP THE SELF-COACHING SESSION.

CASE STUDY

This is a continuation of a client who started with the statement of "I don't know." He came to me every week drowning. There was always something new, something big, something overwhelming him. He was constantly drowning and never seemed to have a moment of reprise.

It started with work first. Then the added responsibilities of caring for a sick mother and an elderly father. And then his partner and wife got terribly sick, and he shouldered all the childcare duties of three young children and the household chores.

He was panicking and overwhelmed. I asked him what he would like to have instead, and he didn't know. I supported him to use a visualization technique to break up his "I don't know" into smaller parts.

He broke them up as:

1. To find a sense of calm.
2. To help his wife and partner fully recover.
3. To strategize how to move forward with all the other responsibilities.

The conversation starts here when I replay back to him the parts of his "I don't know."

I've added my narrative as a coach in italics.

Coach:	I appreciate these three key parts of your I don't know. What makes it important that you broke them up this way?
	Questions of importance allows the expression of values. This is what is important to them.
Client:	I think it's what can bring me peace. Without it, I feel like a chicken running around with its head cut off. I can't make any rational decision. I can't think or function properly. I'm not even sure I can show up as a good boss to my team or even a good father to my children.

Coach: Wow. You want to show up as best as you can. This is why its important to find calm and peace first, because this will allow you to manage everything else.

Client: Oh yes. Yes. Yes, I want to find my inner calm first.

Coach: Wow, to find your inner calm. So, up to now, you know what you would like to have. That is to find a sense of calm, then to support your wife recover, and then strategize how to go from there. What are you learning now?

Client: I think the key is that I have to be in the right headspace to do anything. Without this calm or this inner calm, I can't think straight. Everything is jumbled in my head and overwhelms me. So it's finding this state of calm in any situation. That is what I am learning about myself. This is key for me.

Coach: Wow, I hear that it's so important to find calm in yourself amid times when you feel over-whelmed. And what will you do with this learn-ing?

Client: I think I just need to remind myself that this comes first. Maybe it's paying attention to myself when I become overwhelmed. It doesn't matter what is overwhelming me . . . honestly, as I think about this now, I'm already thinking what to de-prioritize in the house for the next two days as my wife recovers. I may even for-go some of the children's activities. And then, my mom, we can get a plan in place. And work . . . well, I think it's time to be upfront about my mom's situation and just tell them.

Coach:	That is amazing! It sounds like you are already accessing a state of calm right now.
Client:	Yes!
Coach:	And how will this learning that calm is such a critical state for you in managing feeling overwhelmed serve you going forward?
Client:	I guess now that I know, I need to work on myself first. Yes, that's it. I keep thinking only if this would go away or that would disappear, but I know they won't. This is my life. So, I guess part of it is really to focus on myself first and then I will be able to manage. Or even, delegate or just say no. But at least, I've figured a way to take some stuff off my plate.
Coach:	Well done! What would you like to celebrate in yourself today?
Client:	That everything is manageable. I just have to find the calm within. I think I was panicking a little . . . but this has been most helpful.

In the end, the client found both meaningful learning in the session and a way to apply that learning into his life to help him move forward. This is the importance of turning awareness into learning and then into action.

TEACHING MOMENT

Learning is an important part in self-discovery and personal growth. Applied learning is what makes the learning come to life. It allows creation in the form of doing, thinking, or a way of being. A new you. As you learn, you integrate that learning into yourself, and you become a new you. There is no right or wrong way to learn.

Spend more time living your life than thinking about it.

WRAPPING UP THE SELF-COACHING SESSION

Well done on getting here.

What an experience.

Take a moment to recollect yourself.

Take a few deep breaths.

Well done, truly.

To start ...
Consider what you've learned and how it will serve you.

What will allow you to stay committed to this?

-

-

-

It's nice to think through accountability because while you are encouraged and empowered right now about your desires and how to move forward, there will be times when you will get distracted. This is life!

As we wrap up this session, take a moment to think about your original statement and where you started.

Where are you now relative to that statement?

-

-

-

What did you discover out of today's session?

-

-

-

And finally, how would you like to celebrate yourself now?

-
-
-

Thank you for allowing this to guide, teach, and support you. Thank you for trusting this process, and most of all, thank you for trusting yourself.

This is not the end. This is only the beginning.

While this book ends here, your journey and life carry on.

This is the purpose of this book. It is to enable you to build and develop internal tools that help you grow by yourself. Once you learn a new way to think or a new way to see yourself, you are changed. How much you integrate that change depends on you, but you now know that that ability exists within you. You can't undo the experience. You can't unknow the knowledge. Both the knowledge of the tool and the knowledge of yourself. This is what makes self-coaching so powerful and unlimited. All of it is coming from within you.

TEACHING MOMENT

The final step in a coaching process is to create a way forward for you to move boldly and courageously in possibilities to create the life you want. This includes both how you will move forward and a consideration around accountability and commitment. Take this energy and empowerment to follow what excites you. Learn. Grow. Create.

And to wrap everything into a final present, take a moment to reflect on what you want to celebrate. Whatever that may be. There is always something to celebrate. Even if it's being alive and breathing. This mindset of gratitude is a great practice in life, whether it's done through coaching or not.

You are on the right path. Experience every part of yourself across all the spectrums that life has to offer. A struggle is not without lessons. Discovering fear is not without unveiling what needs to be healed. Rewriting your narrative is not without challenging beliefs, values, and your truth. Letting go of judgment of others is letting go of judgment of yourself.

Lose yourself in love. Love of the process. Love of the experience. Love of life.

Our lives are measured by our experiences and what we've learned. It is an infinite process with infinite possibilities.

NOW FOR A PLAN . . .

A goal without a plan is just a wish.

LEARNING OBJECTIVES OF THIS TOOL:

- Understand the characteristics of what you want to create or build for yourself.
- Consider the building blocks for this creation.
- Evaluate timing and resourcing needs.
- Understand your definition of success.
- Establish a basic project plan that you can start with.

Reflection and understanding are good places to start. However, sometimes, it feels incomplete. We are trained and taught to be creatures of production and outcomes. There are situations or moments when it's useful to have a plan so we can move forward intentionally.

Here are a few guided thought questions to get you started. Write down your answers as needed.

It doesn't have to be perfect. You just need to start. And as with all plans, this will evolve.

It starts by articulating (as best as you can) what it is you'd like to create.

What is it? What does it look like and feel like?

-
-
-

What would the evolution of that creation be from now going forward?

-
-
-

What is the timing of each of the phases you can envision?

-
-
-

What would you need to get you there?

-
-
-

How will you know you're doing (or have done) it right?

-
-
-

Well done! What you now have is a shell of a project, in a sense. You've started to give your idea real legs. This moves the idea from concept to reality. It's a great place to start. You can consider transferring this to a more formal project plan or tracking mechanism so you can continue to evolve the plan as you move into execution.

NOW IS A GOOD TIME TO GO TO PAGE 242, WHAT ARE YOU LEARNING NOW?

CASE STUDY

Joanne approached me through a mutual contact on LinkedIn. She engaged me to have some coaching, particularly around setting up a content creation business parallel to her full-time job. She loved baking and experimenting with fusion flavors. We had a few sessions to narrow down her ideation, platform strategy, and delivery model. She was very excited about it, working on branding and some of the social media and marketing concepts, and trialing a few production tools. We ended the coaching engagement there and celebrated her progress over the last few months.

I checked up on Joanne half a year later, only to discover that she'd made minimal progress since our last coaching session. She admitted that work had taken over and she was finding it hard to drive her project forward, even though she was committed to it and still passionate in this space. She was still baking occasionally on the weekends as her de-stress activity, but she struggled to produce and publish content. We reengaged for a few sessions to focus on execution. This is where it mattered to her the most at this time.

We first explored what execution would look like for her. How did she know she was doing this right? From a business perspective, it's often called "the key success factor," but in layman terms, it's basically, how will you know you're doing it right? And then we explored resourcing and investment options. How could she make it happen? We ended up with a business model where she would outsource production and publishing to an agency. Together, we built the structural framework of a plan to get the business model up and running. What was needed? How would she source what she needed? How much was she willing to fund? How much time could she carve out to bake and film given her busy schedule? What was she willing to hold herself accountable for?

This was an important part of her business plan. The executional plan. It would be tracked monthly. From there, I introduced her to a group of other Mommy entrepreneurs, and she joined our monthly accountability group, sharing her progress, where she was stuck, and equally giving back to the group in encouragement and pointers.

It's been six months since, and Joanne's found so much joy in her passion and sharing it with the world. I'm a loyal follower, so I can see her weekly posts and how she is building great momentum in doing what she loves and loving what she does. It's such a beautiful journey to experience this with and through someone!

TEACHING MOMENT

This is giving structure to your thinking so you can understand what it is you're creating, and the resources and timing needed to create it. This is where coaching intentionally blends learning into application. It is taking your internal reflection, understanding it, and allowing you to create something external and real in the outside world. It's an important bridge between inception to reality.

This type of thinking is more logical than reflective in nature. Humans are trained from birth to "do" more than "feel" or "be." We are taught to create with our hands. We are taught to build tangible things. We are taught to produce. This is often the layer of the iceberg that we can see, in ourselves, in others, in the world. There is nothing wrong with only accessing this layer of resources, and sometimes, it is necessary.

It is common that to become excited about ideas, we are motivated. We are keen to get started. And yet, so many of these ideas are just that—ideas. Ideas, especially business ideas, are some of the easiest things to generate sometimes when it comes to human beings. We can do it in the shower or on the toilet. We can do it with friends over dinner or in a business meeting—and we can get so excited about it. Except, bringing an idea into full fruition takes more than sitting on a toilet. It takes intention and commitment. It doesn't matter how small or large a step is; it just has to be in service to your idea. And you repeat this over and over again until you've got something tangible that you're happy with. The growth is in the process, not the outcome. We learn when we are experiencing the ups and downs, the difficults and the easys, the goods and the bads—not when we are given what we want.

Be in love with the progress, not the outcome.

I SEE MYSELF—NOW WHAT?

This is a collection of deeper inquiries to expand your self-awareness. It is useful if you have material to work with in which you can see how you're showing up, such as paper or audio evidence. It is an extension of a self-coaching session and can be used any time you observe these in yourself and your responses.

If you've integrated these in the middle of your session, you can go back to your session to complete the self-coaching. If you've use this at the end of your session, you can go to page 242, WHAT ARE YOU LEARNING NOW? to create more reflective learning.

What observations are you noticing about yourself?	Further inquiries to ask yourself to expand self-awareness
Is there a **word that repeats**? What is the word?	What does this word mean to you? What about this word makes it so significant now?
What types of **punctuation** are used? Are there any that stand out more?	What do these punctuations mean to you? What do these punctuations allow to come forward? How do these punctuations allow you to show up now?
What types of **expressions** are used? Are there any that stand out more?	What do these expressions mean to you? What do these expressions allow to come forward? How do these expressions allow you to show up now?

Is there a **repetitive feeling or emotion** that emerges?

How did it show up?

What did you do with this feeling or emotion?

Can you name it?

Can you describe it?

Where are you now with this feeling or emotion?

Did you notice any **physical reactions**?

What are those physical reactions?

Were there any **parts of your body** that stood out?

For the parts that stood out, what did you feel there?

Thinking back on those reactions, is there any correlation to that reaction with a certain thought, feeling, or emotion?

(For example, some people hold their breath without realizing it when they are angry.)

WORKSHEETS AND QR CODE

WORKSHEETS

THESE ARE THE SELF-COACHING SESSIONS WITH WORKSHEETS:

Use this QR code to access the full-page printer-friendly worksheets.

- **I have an idea (working page)**
- **I feel angry (working page)**
- **I am lost (working page)**
- **I don't know is bigger than me (working page)**
- **I don't know about I don't know (working page)**

fEMPOWER Publications Inc. is a boutique publishing house and community serving purpose-driven women in the pursuit of big dreams. We offer full-service book production and publication, thought-leadership development programs, and collaborative writing opportunities for females of all ages.

www.fempower.pub

 @fempower.pub
 @fempower.pub

Join the Author{ity} Membership